ORDNANCE SURVEY
LEISURE GUIDE
NEW FOREST

Produced jointly by the Publications Division of the
Automobile Association and the Ordnance Survey

Editor Donna Wood
Editorial contributors Michael Cady, Peter
Carne, Derrick Knowlton, Margaret Parsons,
Roger Prebble, Roger Thomas

Original photography Robin Fletcher
Stock photographs ARDEA, Automobile
Association Publications Division Photographic
Library, Sdeuard Bissêrot, BIOFOTOS, Mansell
Collection, PRESS-TIGE

Design The New Book Factory, London
Phototypesetting Parkway Group, London and
Abingdon

Colour Origination by Chelmer Litho Reproduction

Printed and Bound in Great Britain
by Purnell and Sons (Book Production) Ltd.,
Paulton, Bristol

Illustrations Anthony Maynard
Maps extracted from the Ordnance Survey's
Outdoor Leisure Series, with the permission of Her
Majesty's Stationery Office. Crown Copyright
Reserved.

Additions to the maps by the Cartographic Unit of
the Automobile Association.

Produced by the Publications Division of the
Automobile Association.

Distributed in the United Kingdom by the
Ordnance Survey, Southampton, and the
Publications Division of the Automobile
Association, Fanum House, Basingstoke,
Hampshire RG21 2EA.

ISBN 0 86145 150 3 (softback)   AA Ref 56643
ISBN 0 86145 174 0 (hardback)   AA Ref 56685

Published by The Automobile Association and The
Ordnance Survey

A note to campers: those sites marked Forestry
Commission sites carry fewer amenities than those
classified by the AA.

*The picture on the preceding page shows a wild gladiolus — one
of the Forest's rare plants.*

Contents

Welcome to the Forest

*All the major towns and villages
feature in this practical
guide to the New Forest, which
combines the
Ordnance Survey's acclaimed
'Outdoor Leisure' map
with the AA's research and
gazetteer expertise.
Telling the story of the Forest
from its beginnings as
a royal hunting ground nine
centuries ago,
the book traces the customs
and folklore of the area,
while a series of detailed walks
reaches into the heart
of the Forest.
Of interest as much to seasoned
country lovers as first-time
visitors to the area,
this book explores
Britain's history through the
life and times of Nature's most
industrious factory
– the forest tree.*

The Story of the Forest

Those who use the term 'New Forest' are, strictly speaking, liable for prosecution under the Trade Descriptions Act on two counts, for it describes an area which is neither new nor a forest in the generally accepted sense of the word. There are, though, sound historical precedents behind the name. It derives from the Norman-French *Nova Foresta*, a title given to this substantial section of southern England in the years following the Norman Conquest of 1066.

Even at that time, the name was hardly appropriate, for the so-called 'forest' consisted largely of open heath and gorselands. Perhaps the true character of this unique, diverse slice of English countryside, with its many contrasting – some would say conflicting - constituent parts, can never be captured in a few words.

One theme which recurs time and time again in the history and evolution of the Forest is that it has always been 'an area set apart' from the rest of the country. This even extends to the geology of the place, for the Forest lies within the Hampshire Basin, a chalk trough which gradually filled with gravels, sands and clays.

Today, the basic nature of the underlying soil is still very much apparent in the coarse gravel of the Forest drives and the yellow-tinged sand pits which occasionally appear amongst a clump of green conifers. In prehistoric time this thin, poor soil cover hardly made the area an attractive proposition for early settlers, most of whom would have been better accommodated on the low chalk downlands to the north. Yet there is some evidence of the presence of early man on these infertile, difficult lands. Over one hundred Bronze Age round barrows (burial mounds) have been traced, together with scant remains of the Iron Age and Roman times.

Already set apart by its geology, this area further added to its special reserve status in 1079, a crucial (though sometimes disputed) date in the history of the New Forest. Recently arrived from France and firmly established at nearby Winchester, William took stock of his newly-conquered lands in the famous Domesday Book, completed in 1086. Before that, he had apparently decided to acquire, for his own purposes, a huge area of land to the south-west of Winchester, extending as far as the coastline now occupied by the resort of Bournemouth.

His purposes were quite straightforward. He had no major plans for his *Nova Foresta*. To describe this newly-created area as a royal pleasure park would perhaps be too glib – though that, in fact, was just what it was, his own private deer-hunting preserve.

In that one act in 1079, the New Forest established its separate, independent identity. From then on, it was regarded as a place set apart in more ways than one. For a start, it had its own boundary, or perambulation, which in early times was considerably larger than the one that applies today. In broad terms, William's original perambulation ran from Salisbury to Southampton Water, across to Bournemouth and back up the River Avon to Salisbury. (Today's Forest perambulation, enclosing some 148 square miles, is a shrunken version of the ancient boundary since it avoids, for example, the modern developments along the south coast.)

William's so-called 'forest' was better-known, and more accurately described, as the 'furze waste', furze being a local term for gorse. The royal forest was anything but an area of uninterrupted, sylvan woodlands. Mighty oaks and silver-barked beeches were conspicuous by their absence in a landscape which in the main consisted of open heath, grasslands and gorse-covered moors, with only a patchy covering of woods in the north.

To protect his new hunting grounds and the all-important deer which were to provide his sport, the King introduced Forest Law, a strict and savage legal code which removed the rights of the unfortunate peasants within the perambulation. Anything that interfered with the pursuits of royal pleasure (something synonymous with the pursuits of deer) was dealt with quite viciously. Bows and arrows were outlawed, along with the setting of

Fresh, green beech heralds spring in Puckpits Inclosure

traps for deer and hunting at night. Thanks to these measures, the deer of the New Forest became one of the world's first protected species, though it is difficult to look upon William and his royal successors as early conservationists.

More significantly, under the hated Forest Law, commoners were not permitted to enclose land of their own, since fencing and other physical barriers would only interfere with the hunt. In recompense, they were given the common right to allow their domestic animals – their ponies, cattle and pigs – the free run of the forest for grazing. Unfortunately, these animals, together with the thousands of deer, had an adverse effect on the vulnerable woodlands, preventing natural regeneration by damaging young growth and saplings.

By the later Middle Ages, there developed a very persuasive reason to encourage tree growth – an increasing demand for wood as a building material. Animals, the main culprits in destroying young trees, would in future be banished from parts of the Forest.

The first inclosure act was passed in 1482. Soon, large areas of the Forest were enclosed so that new woodlands could become established. The New Forest had entered another phase in its evolution, for in comparing William I's 11th-century inclosure of the entire area to the piecemeal 15th-century inclosures within the overall perambulation, we can detect a fundamental shift in attitude to the area. The royal deer park was becoming increasingly important as a timber-producing area, especially for its prized oakwoods. William, the first – albeit coincidental – wildlife conservationist, was succeeded by later monarchs who became, quite deliberately and methodically, the first woodland conservationists. The 1482 act is important as the first serious attempt to reconcile interests which were in conflict. The complex character of the New Forest, with its increasingly intricate web of competing rights and privileges – woodland versus wildlife, commoner versus Crown – was beginning to emerge.

On the legal and administrative side, changes had also taken place. The early draconian Forest Law had been thankfully relaxed by the Charter of the Forest in 1217, described as the Forest's 'equivalent

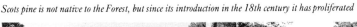

Scots pine is not native to the Forest, but since its introduction in the 18th century it has proliferated

to the Magna Carta'. Commoners could now at least sleep easy in the knowledge that offences could not be punished by mutilation or death. Other less dramatic improvements included a greater protection for the rights of common grazing, the freedom to make certain improvements to private land, and amnesties for past offences.

The administration of justice, even in those days, required the appointment of officials and the creation of a clearly-understood judicial system. Within the Forest, this was based around the Court of the Verderers, a unique institution that survives today.

The ancient Court of the Verderers still sits at Queen's House in Lyndhurst, the little town acknowledged as the 'capital' of the New Forest. It is probably the oldest surviving court in the country, for it must have been established 900-odd years ago when the Forest was first enclosed. The term Verderer comes from the Norman 'vert' (the 'green' of the woodlands) and was used to describe the royal officials who acted for the Crown. Offences were dealt with by a judiciary with a hierarchy of three courts, the most important of which was the Court of the Chief Justice in Eyre, a travelling Forest Court.

Just as the forest laws have survived by changing with time and circumstance, so too have the Verderers. Even though their travelling court may have disappeared, the Verderers still sit six times a year at Lyndhurst. Appointed on a more democratic basis than of old, their main functions are now more administrative and concerned with protecting the rights of the commoner.

The survival of this arcane, medieval institution, with its opening cry of 'Oyez, oyez, oyez!', is emblematic of the tenacity, resilience, and sheer survivability of the Forest as a whole. William the Conqueror may have initiated this process of survival. But without the will and wit to meet new challenges and threats, the Forest could easily have disappeared.

Within this context, the first inclosures of the late 15th century created an important precedent. Inclosures of parcels of land for new timber growth continued for the next few centuries, no doubt encouraged by the burgeoning demand for timber, the main raw material of the time. This led, in 1698, to the passing of the crucial Act of Parliament which allowed the 'rolling power' of inclosure, entitling the Crown to the inclosure of a maximum of 6,000 acres of woodland. This, in effect, was a theoretical maximum for as inclosures matured they could be declared re-open, their acreage then transferred to a new, previously un-enclosed area – an arrangement advantageous to the Crown foresters but understandably unpopular with the commoners.

The Forest's original role as a royal hunting ground was by this time almost forgotten. Indeed, James II appears to have been the last sovereign to exercise his royal hunting rights here in the late 17th century. The Forest was changing in profile and purpose. Trees and the production of timber became the overriding consideration, especially since a new source of demand had recently established itself. The first recorded use of New Forest oak for naval ships can be traced to 1611. Properly seasoned oak from a tree not less than one hundred years old, 'tough, bending well, strong and not too heavy, nor easily admitting water', was ideal for ship construction. Supplies were sent to the naval dockyards in Portsmouth, one large warship consuming 60 acres of trees to give it its much-

An ancient oak; one of the monarchs of the Forest

vaunted heart of oak. Between 1745 and 1818, 50 ships were built at Buckler's Hard on the edge of the forest near Beaulieu, including HMS *Agamemnon* which served in the Battle of Trafalgar.

Throughout these times, the Crown came increasingly into dispute with the commoners, who saw their ancient rights as being eroded through inclosures and the new rolling powers. Their most important right was that of the 'Common of Pasture', which granted the grazing rights to all open lands. Other benefits which commoners might enjoy included the 'Common of Pannage' (the right to allow pigs to forage within the autumn woods for acorns and beech-mast), the 'Common of Turbary' (the right to cut turf for fuel) and the 'Common of Estovers' (the right to collect firewood).

From the early 17th century, contention and argument led to the establishment of a number of Parliamentary Select Committees, today's legacy of which is a definitive collection of records relating to the maze of claims and counter-claims that went before public hearings. Everything is so well documented that it is possible to identify precise cases and resolve existing disputes by reference to old records.

We can trace, for example, rights relating to land located at Annie Down, near Marchwood, once owned by James Holley. His 'Common of Pasture' was for 'All commonable animals, except sheep' and his 'Common of Pannage – For all hogs'. He was also granted 'Common of Turbary and Estovers' and enjoyed 'Other Rights' over 'peat, furze and fern'.

In understanding the history, development and current character of the Forest, it is necessary to see beyond the often comic, certainly rustic content of the ancient rights. Today, they may not be, in straightforward economic terms, as important as they once were. Yet without them, it is unlikely that the New Forest, as a mixed economy and environment, would have survived. The work of the 'four-legged lawnmowers' was, and still is, crucial in preventing the many open areas from becoming overgrown. 'If the animals were to go, in 20 years the New Forest would be all woodland', stated one forest official. Another expert describes the commoners' ponies, horses and cattle as 'the architects of the Forest's scenery'.

Deer, of course, can also be included within this four-legged design staff, although their numbers are now far less than they once were. With the decline in importance of hunting, the earlier, larger herds came to be regarded as unnecessary nuisances who damaged and destroyed young trees. In 1851 the Deer Removal Act was passed, an ambitious piece of legislation that proved quite impossible to implement. The deer, like everything else associated with this ancient forest, seem to have unnatural powers of survival, having weathered royal slings and arrows and parliamentary proclamations. Today, the herds are stabilised at around 1,500, most of which are fallow deer.

While the deer had been fighting their own battle for survival, there had been a change in the look of the Forest. Up until the middle of the 18th century, the Forest woods, glades and timber inclosures had consisted of deciduous hardwoods – oak and beech in the main. From the 1770s, those 'dark foreigners', the faster-growing softwood conifers, were introduced into the Forest.

Gradually, the Forest's old heart of oak was modified by the whiff of pine and the colour of the perennial evergreen. Although both tree types co-exist in harmony here, their characteristics and habitats could not be more different. An oak wood is a fecund, prolific place, supporting around 4,000 living species. Likened by some to an elderly, rather resolute Victorian patriarch, the oak itself requires careful nursing during its growth and has a lifespan of around 200 years. Some will live to 350 and beyond. The conifer, by comparison, is the young, insensitive upstart, with a terminal age of about 120 years, growing quickly and relatively easily in poor soil conditions. The impression of a pine woodland

A fallow doe; part of the 'four-legged design staff'

as a dark, acidic place is only partially correct, for it will contain approximately 1,000 species of animal life.

With the introduction of the Scots pine and other evergreen inclosures, some of the old inclosed areas of oak and beech gradually became part of the untamed open forest. Today, these stately, beautiful, mature woodlands, the epitome of our romantic vision of the medieval forest, are classified under the grand-sounding title of Ancient and Ornamental Woodlands. With their irregular but harmonious growth patterns, their leafy glades and variegated foliage, they stand apart from the more disciplined rows of pines within the modern timber-producing inclosures. Although possibly the result of the very early inclosure movement themselves, the Ancient and Ornamental Woodlands are now developing as natural oak and beechwood, and are classified as 'the finest relics of relatively undisturbed deciduous forest in Britain and probably in the lowlands of western Europe'.

The statutory inclosures containing half coniferous timber and half broad-leaved trees, all the ancient plantings of oak and beech and the open Ancient and Ornamental Woodlands are two of the three main ingredients of the Forest as it now exists. The third is the open heath, grassland and bog. First-time visitors to the New Forest will be surprised by the extent of these windy, treeless plateaux which seem more reminiscent of a Scottish moorland, particularly in August and early

Ponies and cattle 'shading' at Latchmore Bottom

Glades of golden beech in Mark Ash Wood

September when the moors are covered in a purple carpet of bell and common heather. Neither is the archetypal English landscape much in evidence here during the spring and early summer, when dazzling clusters of yellow gorse give the heath the appearance of a county in south-west Ireland.

Most people are surprised to discover that over one-third of the Forest's overall 93,000 acres is taken up by this open heath and grassland. When they leave it though, most visitors will take with them as much an impression of the Forest's wide, open, empty spaces as its arboreal splendour.

Timber inclosures now account for around 22,000 acres, Ancient and Ornamental 8,000, and there are about 26,000 acres of private land used for residential and agricultural purposes. Although they may hint at it, these bald statistics can do little to convey the immense variety of influences and demands that exist, sometimes in opposition, sometimes in equilibrium, within the modern perambulation. Overall responsibility for the Forest now lies with the Forestry Commission, and we may be forgiven for assuming that timber production is the Commission's main concern. Nationally, it unquestionably is. Within the New Forest, the Commission has to play the onerous role of custodian as well as commercial forester, managing a complex mixed economy of woodlands and open heath, recognising the ancient rights of local residents and the demands of casual visitors, whilst at the same time not forgetting their more orthodox responsibilities as measured by the profit and loss equations of 20th-century timber production.

The basis for the modern management of the Forest was established even before the Commission itself was created. The New Forest Act of 1877 limited the Crown's powers of inclosure, abolishing the elastic rolling principle completely. Another milestone in the Forest's history was the Act's recognition of the amenity value of the area as a place of great beauty. This evolution of the official attitude to the Forest – from early game park to timber-producing woodland to a precious part of our national heritage – is interesting to trace, for it reflects the growth and increasing sophistication in our own society from medieval to modern times.

The Forestry Commission assumed responsibility for this far from conventional forest in 1924. As well as dealing with the day-to-day demands of the millions of trees under their care, they also have to accommodate an annual influx of millions of visitors who, if not properly catered for, would soon provide further evidence in support of the first principle of mass tourism: those who come in search of peace and tranquillity tend to destroy what they find.

The phenomenon of recreation on a vast and previously undreamed-of scale has posed a major threat to the New Forest. And a phenomenon it is. In the summer of 1965, the New Forest received 85,000 campers. That figure has now risen to 800,000. The campers, of course, are merely in the vanguard of a much larger army of day visitors and holidaymakers, whose numbers total six-and-one-half to seven million per annum. As one forest officer observed, 'We manage both visitors and trees here'.

The management policies are thoroughly, even fastidiously applied, though they remain surprisingly unobtrusive. Most visitors, for example, arrive by car and soon become aware of shallow but effective ditches and occasional low barriers between the road and open lands, denying any form of four-wheel access. Then again, visitors will not fail to be impressed by – and, more important, accommodated in – any of the many official car parking areas, most of which will have other facilities such as picnic areas as well as serving as the starting point for waymarked Forest walks.

Campers at Holidays Hill

This policy of creating car-free areas by physically preventing vehicles from leaving the roads is central to the conservation of woodland and wildlife. The creative management of visitors is essential, and the Forestry Commission has developed an understanding of the psychology and behaviour-patterns of the car-borne tourist.

Officials will distinguish, for instance, between two basic categories, as defined by 'parkers' and 'visitors'. The former will only under extreme provocation or temptation venture more than a few yards from their parked vehicle. Many of them may never even set foot on Forest soil. The latter attract considerably more respect, for these are seen as the *true* visitors, – a status achieved by one or more of the Forest walks on offer.

The success of these policies is measured by the fact that most visitors (and, presumably, parkers) are quite unaware of the subtle management and monitoring processes to which they are subjected. It may all appear a little sinister, but it is also necessary. Pressure points can quickly be identified, fragile parts of the Forest protected, wildlife, woodland and heath preserved for future generations. Conservation has become a watch-word here. The Forest, home of many rare species of flora, fauna, reptile, bird and insect, is now recognised as a National Nature Reserve, the Forestry Commission undertaking to consult with the Nature Conservancy Council on all relevant issues. The Forest also continues to be the home of the commoners' animals, which, unlike the timorous deer, are still to be found everywhere, particularly in the form of recalcitrant and unmoving groups of ponies dozing in the middle of the road quite impervious to the traffic chaos they have created all around them.

About 5,000 animals still roam the open commonable land, under the supervision of the Court of Verderers which appoints its own agents, known as Agisters, to look after the day-to-day work. Farming though, is not as important as it once was. Cattle are still fattened, ponies still bred for sale at the famous sales at Beaulieu Road and elsewhere. But the fact remains that a much smaller number of commoners – a fraction of the old total – now exercise their traditional grazing rights. Many have become part-time farmers with alternative jobs and other sources of income.

Nevertheless, they are still part of the living traditions of the Forest. They have survived, along with the deer, the gnarled oakwoods, the bracken, bog and moorland. Today, the Forest exercises a powerful hold on our imagination, rekindling images of a once-pastoral Britain clothed with copse, thicket and close. We come to the New Forest not simply because it happens to be there, just down the motorway. We come because we have, as a people, a deep, almost umbilical, relationship with woodland. It is no coincidence that Robin Hood, the man who found sanctuary amongst the trees of the forest, is such an important figure in English mythology and folklore. Shakespeare's bucolic frolic, *A Midsummer Night's Dream*, can be read as our national fairytale.

John Fowles, author of *The French Lieutenant's Woman* and *Daniel Martin*, speculates in the latter novel of the need for such a retreat, 'a place outside the normal world . . . intensely green and fertile, numinous, haunted and haunting, dominated by a sense of magic . . .'. This may seem too fanciful a notion for some, especially when trapped in Lyndhurst's traffic jams on a hot summer's day. Yet

The sundew grows on the wet heaths of the Forest, and traps small insects to supplement its diet

the appeal of the New Forest must largely be based on its status as a surviving slice of medieval, if not merrie, England. Its place names – Ferny Knap, Dames Slough, King's Garn Gutter Inclosure – awaken a buried sense of times gone by. Its arcane traditions and clannish little communities where long-standing residents of over 20 years are still regarded as outsiders, speak of a self-sufficient, almost closed society which is bound to be a source of endless fascination to the big, bland world outside.

Most of all, there is the visual appeal of the forest and moorland, surviving remnants from an older, earlier age, set in a landscape of great natural beauty. The New Forest has survived because it has always been this special place, set apart from the rest of the country. Its royal status as Crown land and its traditional code of laws insulated it against the pressures which might otherwise have destroyed it. It is also special in having been managed throughout its entire 900-year history, whether as a consequence of the selfish motives of the early Normans or the far-ranging responsibilities of the Forestry Commission. Although its basic character as an inviolate wilderness is presently stable and secure, it is salutary to remember that this is a delicately-balanced area. A motorway now ends within a few miles of Lyndhurst. Petro-chemical stacks prick the horizon on the Forest's eastern fringe. Densely-populated south coast resorts and the London metropolis are just a short car journey away. We must, for the future, continue to avoid the complacent observation that the New Forest is a born survivor.

Pony-trekking is a popular pursuit

A Forest of Folklore

For hundreds of years a wealth of myth and legend has wound itself around the trees of the New Forest like a clinging vine. William the Conqueror started it all in about 1079 when he adopted the 200 square miles of furzey waste and woodland for his own hunting ground, causing great bitterness among many of the inhabitants. Early historians state that in doing so William ruined no fewer than 60 parishes and 36 churches, but this is disputed by later records. Nevertheless, William's reputation for rough justice does seem to be deserved; his forest laws held that after an inquest among the four nearest villages, the penalty for killing a deer was death, for shooting at a deer (but missing) loss of hands, and for disturbing a deer, loss of eyesight! The popular myth that the first forest laws were introduced by King Canute, King of England from 1016 until his death in 1035, has been proved to be based upon a forgery.

It is William II, son of the Conqueror and commonly known as King Rufus, on whom the most famous of New Forest legends is based. This villainous monarch, unpopular with the Church and most of his subjects, met an untimely death while hunting in the Forest in the early evening of 2 August 1100. The Rufus Stone at Canterton Glen commemorates the King's death and supplies a few sentences about how it happened.

Sir Walter Tyrrell, a French nobleman in the King's hunting party, loosed an arrow at a stag, which glanced off the beast's back and struck Rufus in the chest. The strangest thing about this story is the lack of ceremony that followed the death. Sir Walter Tyrrell rode off, poste haste to seek safety in Normandy, pausing only, as legend has it, at the south-east boundary of the Forest to order a blacksmith to put his horse's shoes on backwards, a device to confuse anyone sent to track him down. He need not have bothered. The other members of the hunting party had dispersed in various directions, Rufus' brother Henry to Winchester, to claim the throne, with William de Breteuil close behind him, to make a claim on behalf of the Conqueror's eldest son Robert. Nobody seems to have gone into mourning for Rufus; a fact which led many to believe that the killing was not an accident, but a planned assassination. He was generally disliked, and his description, written by William of Malmesbury, helps us to understand why: 'He was small and thick set and ill-shaped, yet having enormous strength. His face was redder than his hair and his eyes were of two different colours. His vices were branded on his face'. Political ambition is the most probable motive, but other wild rumours held that Tyrrell killed the King because he suspected him of seducing his wife or that Rufus had been 'removed' because he had blocked the marriage of Henry, youngest son of the Conqueror to his love Eadgyth, daughter of the King of Scotland. Perhaps the most outlandish theory, probably inspired by Rufus' devilish looks, was that he was actually a witch king of the Catharist heresy and had willed his own death to atone for the sins of the world.

The legend of Dame Alicia Lisle is a sad affair founded on scanty records. It seems that in the late 17th century this aged and kindly woman sheltered in her New Forest home two rebels who were on the run after the Battle of Sedgemoor, supporters of the defeated Lord Monmouth whom they had hoped to put on the throne. The two fugitives were soon uncovered at the Dame's home, and she was tried by the notorious Judge Jeffreys and sentenced to be burned alive the same afternoon. For some reason a

The Rufus Stone is said to mark the spot where King Rufus fell in 1100

White Hart sign can be seen at Ringwood, where a hunting party including Henry VIII and various gentlemen and women stopped for refreshment after chasing a beautiful white buck through the Forest. At the ladies' request, its life was spared.

A particularly mischievous imp known as Laurence was, in earlier times, a well-known Forest dweller, with the power to make men idle or drowsy. A lazy peasant in the 17th century would be said by his New Forest friends to have a 'touch of Laurence'. Shakespeare was thought by many to have based his creation of Puck on another sprite dwelling in the Forest, whose chief delights were causing colts to stray and drawing people into the bogs, laughing at their plight, and turning himself into hundreds of different shapes. Only the first born child in a family was exempt from Puck's caprices. The Forest placenames reflect the strong belief in these legends in early times; with Puck's Hill at Prior's Acre, and not far from there the great wooded Puckpits Inclosure, an enchanting mass of tangled oaks and beeches. Pixey Field, Pixey Mead and Puck's Piece are also in the area.

The Priory Church of Christchurch on the south-west border of the Forest was originally planned for St Catherine's Hill, a lonely site quite impractical for the needs of the people living down in the valley. By day workmen following their orders lugged the great stones for the building up the hill, only to find them at the bottom again the next day; moved during darkness by some unseen hands or supernatural force. Naturally, the plans were changed and the people got their church where they wanted it. The workmen reported feeling a Divine Presence among them, speeding up the building process.

Scores of Kings, Queens, peasants, gypsies, smugglers, murderers and lovers have passed through the New Forest in 900 years and it is little wonder that such colourful people have inspired such colourful legend. Yet it is only one of many ways in which the New Forest is unique.

The white buck is a beautiful freak in the fallow deer family

stay of execution was obtained and Dame Alicia was able to petition James II for clemency. The King showed some mercy, but was not over generous; the death method, but not the sentence, was changed and she was beheaded at Winchester soon after. Her simple grave can be seen at Ellingham churchyard, from where, on certain dark nights, her ghost has been sighted, being driven in a wagon with headless horses and no driver, back to her home at Moyles Court.

The white buck, whose image is seen so often on pub signs, is in reality a very rare and beautiful animal, which comes into being only occasionally, due to some unknown phenomenon in the genes of the fallow deer. Legend has it that the original

Christchurch Priory, Dorset, where 'unseen hands' were said to have taken part in the building work

The Farmyard Forest

Horseriding in Aldridge Hill Inclosure

Ponies have ranged freely through the New Forest for countless centuries. They were here when William the Conqueror made the region his favourite playground and for an unknown period before that, so that their origins are lost to us. They may well have always lived in this lovely corner of southern England, ever since genuinely wild ponies roamed the primeval forests of a Britain which had yet to be tamed and trammelled by man.

Are today's ponies truly wild, though? With their unkempt manes and shaggy tails, their stocky build so ideally suited to the environment where they and their forebears have lived and flourished for so long, they are as much a part of the Forest's natural scene as the very woods and heathery moors which are their home. Yet they all have owners.

These are the New Forest commoners, whose rights to turn out domestic livestock date back to a time when the fencing of agricultural holdings was not permitted as this would interfere with the free movement of the King's deer throughout the Forest.

Common rights of pasture still go with the ownership or tenancy of many farms and smallholdings in and around the New Forest area. Sometimes they have been enjoyed by the same families for many generations, with the result that there exists a special breed of men for whom the exercising of New Forest common rights is a way of life demanding particular skills and knowledge of the unique tract of country where they and their animals have their home.

Need for this knowledge arises when they ride out on to the Forest to help with the regular round-ups, or 'drifts', as these are called in New Forest language. The purpose of these drifts is to herd the ponies and other free-ranging livestock into pounds – or 'corrals', in Wild West parlance – for marking with their owners' individually registered brands and for the selection of some animals for sale.

Another reason for the drifts is the annual collection of what are known as marking fees for each animal, to cover the cost of overseeing and administering common rights. The officials responsible for this, and also for keeping an eye on the general welfare of 'commonable' animals while these are at liberty in the Forest, are known as Agisters – a medieval title which in modern English means simply 'collectors'.

Four Agisters divide the 45,000 acres of New Forest grazing land between them, and each has his own individual way of clipping hair from the tail of every pony for which a marking fee has been paid. This enables all the ponies to be individually checked to confirm their right to be on the Forest, and the area where they were rounded up and tail-marked can be identified at the same time.

While constantly patrolling the Forest on horseback, the Agisters keep a wary eye open for ponies and other livestock in trouble. Every spring some ponies are tempted by the 'early bite' of molinia grass which grows in the numerous bogs to wander into these treacherous areas. They often sink in up to their bellies and will soon drown unless hauled out - by no means an easy task, as may be imagined, but one which the Agisters have to be able to cope with.

Until the mid 1960s nearly all New Forest roads were unfenced. This meant that even the busiest highways could be crossed at will by the ponies, all too often with fatal consequences. Animal fatalities have been more than halved as a result of the subsequent fencing of all major roads. Unfenced roads leading into and out of the Forest have had cattlegrids installed to prevent ponies straying, the result of a special Act of Parliament.

Ponies were part of the Forest before William I enclosed it

Secondary and unclassified roads in the Forest remain unfenced. On all of them special care still needs to be taken to avoid accidents involving livestock. Semi-wild ponies near the regular haunts of man become very trusting, and visitors seeing them for the first time may be tempted to offer them food. This is not only illegal, incurring the risk of a heavy fine, but encourages animals to stray on to the roads where they become a danger to traffic – and to themselves.

Dealing with animal casualties on the roads remains one of the most frequent, and least pleasant, of the Agisters' many tasks. They carry humane killers to end the misery of victims clearly beyond veterinary care. Veterinary surgeons themselves help check on animals at large that may be in poor health for various reasons.

Only the strongest survive a severe New Forest winter

New Forest ponies are in general hardy beasts with good health records. Many do well on a winter diet which includes large amounts of gorse and other rough herbage which animals reared in a softer environment would refuse. Even so, winter is a season when 'poor doers' are particularly vulnerable. Any noted are reported via the Verderers to the Agisters, who have power to order their removal to the holdings of their owners.

The New Forest Court of the Verderers is a picturesque survival from times when a special code of forest laws protected the King's game from poachers and its habitat from encroachment. Its purpose today is to administer common rights and to deal with any problems which might arise. The Court consists of five members appointed to represent various official bodies and five others, elected from their number, by the commoners themselves. It meets bi-monthly, on a Monday, in the Verderers' Courtroom at Lyndhurst.

Pigs at pannage—Wessex saddlebacks in Bramshaw Wood

A skewbald donkey and foal at Stoney Cross Plain

As well as some 3,000 ponies, two score or so donkeys enjoy a free life in the Forest, under the Verderers' jurisdiction. Owned like the ponies by various commoners, these make a picturesque addition to the life of the areas they frequent, especially in early summer when accompanied by their newly-born young.

Much more important economically are the cattle turned out on the Forest. In recent years these have fluctuated in numbers from around 1,600 to something like double that figure, though many are taken in by their owners in winter. Like the ponies, they may be seen grazing in nearly all parts of the open Forest, though they tend to avoid the more heavily wooded areas. Many ponies, on the other hand, spend much of their time in dense woodland, often penetrating the large forestry inclosures which are supposed to be fenced against them.

Something more substantial than ordinary stock fencing is required to keep out pigs turned loose to fatten on acorns and beechmast. One of the most ancient of all common rights, this is still widely used by New Forest commoners during what is called the 'pannage' season. Formerly this lasted from 25 September to 22 November, but can now be varied to provide a minimum of 60 days' pannage at a time when the nut crop is deemed sufficiently abundant to provide the maximum benefit.

Perhaps the most colourful of all those events that arise from the presence of commonable animals on the Forest are the pony sales held several times a year near Beaulieu Road station. Most animals thus disposed of end up as children's riding ponies, for which there is a big demand not only in Britain itself but from overseas.

Aristocrats of the Forest

especially poaching, were often severe in the extreme, and were inflicted by forest courts convened at intervals specifically for the purpose of trying offenders against the 'vert' (the timber and its environment) and the 'venison', or game. Thus came about the beginnings of what is still called the Verderers' Court or, more correctly, the Court of Swainmote and Attachment which, however, now has a function more in keeping with present day needs in relation to commoners and their rights.

A white buck takes pride of place in this herd of fallow deer, with their dappled summer coats

Most sought after of all by many visitors to the New Forest is a view of its deer. These have a very special local importance because, without them, there would never have been a forest here in the first place. It is recorded of William the Conqueror that 'he loved the tall deer as if he were their father'. He certainly loved the hunting of them, and it was for this very purpose that, in or around 1079, he set aside this region – which he then named the 'New' Forest – for the preservation of deer in order that he and his guests might hunt them whenever he chose to take leave from the more everyday cares of kingship.

A special set of forest laws was superimposed on the ordinary laws of the land to ensure that the sovereign's wishes were carried out in every detail. No man might fell timber, clear a few acres for agriculture, or even protect what farmland he already had from the hungry mouths of deer intent on sampling his crops.

No man living in the Forest might keep a dog, except a very small one, without having its front claws chopped off ('expeditated' was the term used) to prevent it from chasing and harrying the King's deer. No man might turn out his ponies and cattle to graze during the 'fence month', 20 June to 20 July, when the deer with their newly born fawns were to be left completely undisturbed, or during the 'winter heyning', 22 November to 4 May, when feed was considered to be too scarce to be shared by the deer with other livestock.

Above all, no man might hunt the King's deer without express permission, granted only to a few privileged officials for special purposes.

Penalties for offences against forest law,

As the centuries wore on, royal interest in preserving the deer declined, while the Forest's importance for other uses, particularly the growing of timber and, more recently, as an area for public recreation and for the preservation of plant and animal wildlife for its own sake, progressively increased.

The fortunes of the deer reached their lowest ebb when, in 1851, an Act of Parliament authorised their 'removal'. This was part of a package deal whereby the Crown traded its right to preserve royal game, which was no longer needed, for the right to exclude the commoners' livestock from 10,000 acres in addition to the fairly small area already fenced against ponies and cattle for the purpose of growing trees.

The extra trees were successfully planted and grown, but determined efforts to exterminate the deer ran into difficulties. A great many were slaughtered, but in so extensive an area as the New Forest, with its abundance of dense cover – and with large woods outside the Forest affording sanctuary to such deer as chose to hide there – killing the very last of these lovely animals proved impracticable.

Reduced in the space of two years from several thousand to perhaps a few score, deer lingered on in remoter parts. The desire to bring about their total extinction passed, and eventually they increased again to the point where they were to be seen once more in small numbers in most of their former haunts.

Today some 1,500 deer of five different species are to be found in the New Forest. They are maintained at around this level so as to minimise

A fallow buck in winter pelage

The antlerless females are smaller than the males and tend to keep in separate groups even when the bucks and does are feeding quite close together. Most are dappled fawn on the flanks in summer, changing to chestnut brown in winter, but in the sanctuary area there is quite often a creamy-white deer as well as the odd black individual. Sometimes, one appears that is much lighter-spotted than most of the others and remains dappled all year round.

When you look for these deer in the woods where most of them live, carry binoculars, walk quietly and avoid causing any unnecessary disturbance. Above all, keep your dog on a lead or, better still, leave it at home – and never, never pick up and take home a fawn that seems to be deserted; it is merely lying up in seclusion while its mother goes off to graze, probably not far away.

The broad-palmed antlers of the fallow bucks contrast with the big, branchy headgear of the red deer, largest of all our British wild animals. Once almost extinct in the New Forest, these now occur in moderate numbers and may be encountered, with

Autumn in Mark Ash Wood

damage to farmers' crops, to garden vegetables and flowers, and to forest trees, which would become serious if the numbers of these animals were allowed to increase unchecked.

Old, weak and sickly animals are humanely culled by the New Forest keepers, who are trained to use high-powered rifles for the purpose. Shooting is mostly done at dawn and dusk, when deer are on the move between their feeding and resting places and very few people are about, and deer culling is confined to specified seasons when the antlers of the male deer, shed once a year, are fully regrown, and young deer have reached a stage where they no longer depend on their mothers for milk and other basic requirements.

At Bolderwood, four miles to the west of Lyndhurst, a small former farm in the heart of the Forest has been transformed into a sanctuary where wild deer come and go unmolested. Here, at practically any time, those who may never previously have seen deer of any kind can watch the most plentiful New Forest species, the fallow deer, for as long as they wish, either from an observation tower on the sanctuary's edge or simply by looking over the fence. Visitors may not enter the sanctuary itself – this is just for the deer and their keepers. Feeding them daily ensures their regular presence in the Forest, in fairly large numbers of both sexes.

A young fallow doe

luck, almost anywhere. Red deer, like fallow, live in herds, sometimes of a dozen or more together.

The much smaller roe deer, on the other hand, tend to live in family units of a doe with her fawn or twin fawns of the year, sometimes with a buck also tagging along. Foxy-red in summer, greyish-brown in winter and with conspicuous white rumps but no visible tail, these graceful, agile wanderers through the very deepest woods are widely distributed over the Forest but are not always easy to find. In the early and late hours of the day you may sometimes spot them in the more open parts, but unless you tread very carefully they will probably spot you first, throw up their heels and bound away in a series of effortless undulations.

Midway between fallow and roe deer in size and with antlers almost as impressive as those of the red deer are the sika deer from Japan, introduced early this century. These are mainly to be found in woods to the south of the Southampton–Bournemouth railway, east of Brockenhurst, and are locally quite numerous.

Smallest and most elusive are the muntjac deer, an Asian species that has found a home for itself in Britain. Well established in the Midlands and now extending southward, this spaniel-sized lover of really thick cover can also too easily secrete itself from casual observation, and you will be fortunate to catch sight of one of the very few so far established in the New Forest.

When driving through the Forest keep an especially wary eye open for deer as, unlike the ponies, they are not restrained by ordinary fences and all too frequently meet their deaths, or are badly maimed, in collision with cars.

The Secret Life of the Forest

After deer, the four-footed wild animals most likely to be seen during a casual stroll in the New Forest are squirrels. Forty years ago these would have been our native British red squirrels. However, that transatlantic interloper, the grey squirrel, arrived on the scene in the 1940s and within a few years entirely displaced its indigenous cousin throughout the area.

For all their engaging agility as they make their effortless-seeming way through the highest branches, leaping from one tree to another and only rarely misjudging the distance, it has to be remembered that grey squirrels cause serious damage to growing trees and in private gardens, so their numbers have to be very strictly controlled by the New Forest keepers.

Rabbits were much reduced by the myxomatosis epidemic which first swept the south in the 1950s. They have made a fairly good recovery, but have never been really numerous in the New Forest – which is just as well because they, too, are no friend to the forester. Hares are even less numerous and are inclined to be rather localised, so that in some parts they are almost never seen.

There is always a chance of seeing a fox abroad by day in the quieter parts. When these animals hunt in broad daylight it is usually because they are hungry after an unsuccessful foray the previous night. They like to lie up in the remote recesses of bogs and similar places and will sometimes borrow part of the earth, or 'sett', of a colony of badgers as a safe place to which to retreat for the day or in which to hide their cubs.

The Forest is noted for its badgers. These mostly live in underground fortresses deep in the woods and are almost never seen during the middle hours of the day. To watch them at close quarters it is necessary to wait for badgers to emerge from their setts around dusk – but make sure you arrive in good time because they sometimes begin their nightly wanderings well before dark.

Otters, always elusive, have suffered a serious decline over much of Britain in recent years and rarely visit New Forest streams now. American

The grey squirrel – a transatlantic interloper

Mainly noctrurnal, the red fox makes occasional daytime forays in the Forest in search of food

mink are much more in evidence. Having escaped from fur farms and bred in freedom, these have established themselves in the wild and are present on several New Forest waterways. They are most likely to be seen towards dusk.

Stoats and weasels are scarce. Hedgehogs, for some reason, are hardly ever seen in the Forest, and water voles – commonly misnamed 'water rats' – are virtually absent. The other common voles, mice and shrews of Britain all occur here. These mostly lead their lives in secret to try to escape their numerous predators.

Many a New Forest ride is pimpled from time to time with molehills. As a rule this surface evidence is the only visible sign of the strictly subterranean mole, which annoys gardeners by its persistent tunnellings but is here quite harmless.

As daylight merges into darkness bats take wing. Apart from Leisler's bat and a few very local rarities, all the British species from the large noctule to the small pipistrelle have been recorded here, among them the uncommon barbastelle and still rarer Bechstein's bat.

The risk of encountering venomous snakes deters some people from exploring the New Forest on foot in warmer weather, though the danger of snakebite in fact is very small. Britain's only poisonous species is the common viper or adder. Rarely more than about 18 inches in length, this has a distinctively blunt tail and varies considerably in colour but most specimens have a conspicuous zigzag line all along the body.

Adders prefer dry situations such as heathery slopes and wood-edge banks, where they like to coil up and sun themselves. Highly sensitive as they are to the vibrations of approaching footfalls, they will nearly always vanish underground long before there is any danger of their being trodden upon.

The time to be extra careful is in early spring, when adders are sluggish after first emerging from their winter hibernation and may not always move fast enough to escape being crushed underfoot.

Their instinctive reaction to any such threat, quite naturally, is to strike in self-defence. Even so, snakebite is decidedly uncommon and, in Britain, hardly ever fatal.

Grass snakes, sometimes several feet long and distinguishable from adders by their prominent yellow collar, are harmless and, as a rule, a good

Badgers depend mainly on their keen sense of smell to find food

The pipistrelle bat is found in the Forest

deal more plentiful. They are much more partial than adders to a watery situation and may sometimes be seen hunting for frogs and small fish in streams and bogs.

The rare smooth snake, a kind of miniature boa-constrictor, is also quite harmless and should on no account be interfered with. It vaguely resembles an adder but lacks the warning zigzag line, has twin rows of small dark spots along its back and is very much more slender, lacking the blunt tail of its venomous relative. Sandy heathland with water at hand is the smooth snake's favourite habitat.

A favourite prey of this snake, where available, is the sand lizard, though in the New Forest this has

An adder is recognised by its zigzag markings

become extremely scarce in recent years and may even be extinct now. The common or viviparous lizard, so named because it brings forth living young, is plentiful and widespread, as is the slow-worm, a legless lizard often mistaken for a snake.

A feature common to all these lizards is their facility for detaching a tail when a predator grabs hold of it, and later growing a new one – not quite so long as the tail it replaced.

Specimens of all New Forest reptiles may be seen in the reptiliary by Holidays Hill Cottage, just north of the A35 two miles west of Lyndhurst. Never kill a snake or lizard – they enjoy the same total protection as all other New Forest wildlife apart from the very few harmful species whose numbers the keepers control.

All three British species of newts – common, crested and smooth – are to be found here, as are the common toad and frog.

Small brown trout and various coarse fish flourish in the New Forest streams and ponds and may be fished for, in due season, by those who purchase a special licence.

New Forest insect species are countless and include many interesting specimens. If stinging flies of various kinds are sometimes too common for comfort in summer – when mosquitoes and midges are also a menace to the evening wildlife-watcher – this is more than compensated for by the abundance of beautiful butterflies. You may search in vain for the rare purple emperor, though this has been rather more in evidence in Hampshire in some recent summers, but the white admiral butterfly and the silver-washed fritillary are just two among many other kinds which are almost to be regarded as New Forest specialities.

A silver-spotted Blue; found on heathland

Several species of hawk moths haunt the Forest in due season. Stream courses in high summer are a-dance with dragonflies and damselflies. The timbered expanses themselves support large colonies of wood ants, which harbour in huge mounds of pine needles assembled laboriously by themselves.

Wherever you walk, wherever you look, the wildlife world of the New Forest offers something to catch the eye . . . to entertain you and instruct you in the wonderful ways of nature.

The Forest in Flight

Often heard but not seen, the birds of the New Forest forage for food, swoop silently on to their prey and live their mysterious, unseen lives like highly-trained guerillas in a jungle terrain. They are first recognised by their song, then, if you are lucky enough, or quick enough, by their plumage. An unmusical 'seng, seng, seng', heralds the arrival of the meadow pipit, a typical bird of the ling zone. The skylark, too, is not uncommon on the heathland although more at home in the grassy areas. Superficially it is similar to the meadow pipit, from which it can be distinguished by its less slender build, the presence of a crest and a quite different call-note. The song of the lark is well-known and unmistakable.

The Dartford warbler is protected by law

In a slightly different habitat on the edge of woodland, two close relatives of the last two may occasionally be seen and heard. The commonest is the tree pipit which rises from a tree with a pleasant song easily identifiable after it has been heard a few times. The woodlark has become quite scarce. Its song, often uttered in flight, is a melodic warbling and the obviously short tail is another good identifying feature. It is along the fringes of the wood, too, that you may hear that romantic-sounding bird of the twilight, the nightjar, uttering its strange, ventriloquial churring note. It has, however, become very scarce in recent years.

The areas of gorse have their own distinctive breeds. Three or four slender finch-like birds erupting from the gorse tops at the slightest sound or movement and moving swiftly with undulating flight are likely to be linnets. They are restless birds, gregarious even in the breeding season, often nesting in colonies. The cock bird in his summer plumage of chestnut-brown back, crimson forehead and breast is quite handsome if only he will keep still long enough to be seen! Another bird often perched conspicuously on gorse is the stonechat, a dumpy little fellow with red-brown breast, black head and dark brown back. It constantly flicks its tail and utters a call-note resembling two pebbles being knocked together. A rare bird which is more secretive and tends to skulk in the depths of the gorse making a soft churring note, is the Dartford warbler. Sometimes, however, it appears in the open when its long, well-elevated tail is immediately

noticeable. This species is especially protected by law and must not be disturbed in any way.

A large green bird with red crown and yellowish rump will be the green woodpecker, which often leaves the woods to feed upon the abundant ant population of the heaths. When it flies away you will notice it has a heavy, dipping flight as though the wings are not strong enough to bear the body. Large black birds are more likely to be crows than rooks; they fly over the heathland seeking anything, animal or vegetable, that they can devour. A common sight is a bird of prey hovering motionless in the sky as it patiently watches for small mammals and insects. This is the kestrel or windhover.

The bogs attract other species. The typical small bird is the reed bunting. The cock is brown above and whitish below with a black head and throat and a white collar; his song consists of a jangle of three or four not very tuneful notes. The mallard duck is fairly often seen circling the bogs, and a distinctly smaller duck is likely to be a teal. You may perhaps see a very large grey bird with an enormous bill, standing motionless beside a boggy pool. This will be a visiting heron, waiting with infinite patience for signs of a tasty morsel.

In the spring there are several waders which are a joy to watch and hear. The snipe has an extremely long bill and rises suddenly with a harsh cry. Its courtship display is nothing less than spectacular. The bird soars to a considerable height and then descends steeply with outspread tail. A strange sound is produced by the action of the wind through the tail feathers and this sound has been likened to the bleating of a goat or sheep. It carries for a considerable distance and will often be heard before the bird itself is seen. As it circles, preparing itself for another display, it utters an excited 'chippa, chippa' call.

The redshank is a medium-sized wader with a white rump and a white band at the rear edge of its wings. Several birds will join in the display flight

The female whinchat is a summer visitor to the Forest

The mistle thrush may attack anyone venturing too near the nest

Green woodpeckers of both sexes feed their nestlings

singing a simple but melodious song. The curlew, a large wader with a long curved bill whose call-note mimics its name, will breed in the Forest. Its song is a rapidly accelerating succession of notes terminating in a trill – one of the beautiful and haunting sounds of summer.

Few birds are found in dense coniferous plantations except tits and goldcrests. But where there is a stand of well-spaced mature Scots pine you may come across a curious bird, the crossbill. Your attention may first be drawn to a number of cones being thrown to the ground. Looking up, you may see a small party of birds high up in a tree busily and noisily extracting seeds from the cones. The twisted beak which develops as the young bird grows is specially adapted for this task. The red plumage of the cock contrasts well with the glaucous green of the pine needles but the hen is a dull yellow-green. In flight its short tail is noticeable and as it flies it utters a distinctive call-note 'jup'.

The common birds of deciduous and mixed woodland include tits of several species, wren, robin, blackbird, song and mistle thrushes. The last-named is a characteristic bird of open woods and woodland edge. The shrub layer is insufficient to attract large numbers of summer migrants but the willow warbler and chiff-chaff are common. The willow warbler has a beautiful if plaintive descending cadence of song, while the chiff-chaff monotonously sings its name. A third species of leaf warbler, the wood warbler, is less common but can be heard high up in deciduous trees uttering its shivering trill. In the old woods where holes for nesting are plentiful the lovely redstart, its orange-red tail constantly quivering, may be found.

The trunk-climber belongs to a special group of birds among which are also common species like woodpeckers, nuthatches and tree-creepers. Nuthatches are handsome birds with blue-grey upper parts and a buffish colour underneath. Tree-creepers are mouselike and not so conspicuous.

A loud mewing call above the trees denotes a common buzzard, a large bird of prey with broad wings. They are most readily observed when soaring

on a thermal.

If you are still in the woods when dusk approaches a tawny owl will probably be heard, and possibly a plump wader with an enormous bill, a woodcock, may be seen and heard making its croaking call as it goes on what is called its 'roding' flight. It is hard to think of a more pleasant way to end a day in the New Forest.

Greater spotted woodpeckers are found in almost every mainland county and are often seen and heard in the Forest

The Forest in Flower

As you stroll across a stretch of heathland you will probably notice clumps of gorse, an occasional cluster of graceful silver birches, a sprinkling here and there of Scots pine and possibly a sheltered slope clad with bracken. But the overwhelming mass of vegetation will consist of heather in apparent dull uniformity. The drabness, however, is redeemed in late summer when the landscape takes on a purple glow from the heather bloom.

The uniformity, in any case, is more apparent than real, for there are three kinds of heather growing in the New Forest and in addition a careful look will reveal a variety of delightful tiny flowers growing underneath them. The three heathers occupy slightly different niches within the heathland habitat although there is some overlap.

In the driest spots, especially on banks of plateau gravel, the earliest flowering one of the three will be found. This is bell heather, possibly the most beautiful, whose crimson bells begin to open towards the end of June. In wet hollows the pink-flowered, cross-leaved heath grows and since the leaves are greyer than the others it is quite easy to distinguish. The last species, ling or Scottish heather, is very much the commonest of the three and its rose-purple flowers light up the heathland scene in August.

There are also three kinds of gorse or, as the local inhabitants are more likely to call it, furze. Much the commonest as its name implies is common gorse, a strong-growing shrub up to six feet high. Dwarf gorse, which is fairly plentiful, does not reach such heights. Welsh gorse is quite rare in the Forest, but it does occur in the western part. A dwarf shrub may be seen in early summer with flowers resembling those of gorse but with tiny oval leaves. This will be petty whin, a plant closely related to gorse.

You will need to get on your knees to examine closely the tiny, attractive plants growing amongst the heather. They include heath milkwort which

Wild gladiolus is one of the rarest wild flowers in Britain

may have blue, red or white flowers, heath lousewort with rose-coloured hooded flowers, tormentil, an erect plant with four-petalled yellow flowers and heath bedstraw, a rambling plant with white flowers. An interesting semi-parasitic plant on heather is called the lesser dodder. It looks like a mass of brown thread from which suckers fasten themselves to heather and certain other plants.

Walking near bracken you may smell a sweet scent. A quick search may reveal the lesser butterfly orchid which has white flowers. Under bracken also grows one of the Forest's specialities, the rare and beautiful wild gladiolus. On no account should these, or any plants, be picked or dug up; they are protected by the Wild Creatures and Wild Plants Protection Act, 1975, and by Forest byelaws.

In various low-lying parts valley bogs have been formed, holding a wealth of plants to excite the interest of botanists. The average visitor paying a casual visit is not likely to be properly equipped for any real exploration of these potentially dangerous areas. Forest bogs are easily identifiable from a distance by the white plumes of cotton grass waving in the breeze.

Common on acidic soils throughout the country, tormentil is a member of the rose family

It will still be possible to see something of the flora either from a vantage point such as, for example, where a bridge crosses a sluggish stream, or by skirting the fringes of the bog. There is a fairly distinct zone of vegetation here, consisting of cross-leaved heath, and bog myrtle – an aromatic shrub whose powerful scent gives a characteristic fragrance to the bogs. It is in this zone that the blue flowers of the rare marsh gentian may be seen during August. This is another specially-protected plant – in the past it was used for treating lung diseases. An often-seen and attractive small flower is the bog asphodel, with rich yellow petals and narrow, sword-like leaves. Its common name indicates that it belongs to the lily family but its scientific name *ossifragum* derived from the belief that it made brittle the bones of sheep that ate it. A smaller plant still, just a rosette of leaves on the ground, is the sundew. Of the three species which occur, the round-leaved is the commonest. This is a fascinating plant, for it supplements its diet from the soil by catching insects. The leaves, which are fringed with sticky red hairs, trap insects and then after curling inwards complete the process by digesting the unfortunate creatures. Deep in the bogs in a few places the majestic fronds of the royal fern, so popular with Victorian gardeners, can be seen.

The lesser butterfly orchid rarely exceeds 12 inches, and is found in open woods and grassland

Lousewort occurs on damp heaths and grassland

Covering much of the bog surface, especially around the stems of cotton grass, is the moss known as sphagnum. The leaves consist of hollow cells which absorb moisture like a sponge. This valuable property was put to good use in war-time by the use of vast quantities of these mosses as surgical dressings.

Woodland flowers do not flourish in the dense coniferous plantations where little light penetrates, but rather in the open woods and those parts of the inclosures where deciduous trees are predominant. A typical plant is the wood spurge, with its yellow-green flowers in spring. Anyone familiar with the cultivated spurges or the little garden weed, petty spurge, will have no difficulty in identifying it. The violets growing by the side of the rides are the food of the caterpillars of the various fritillaries, whilst the flowers of bramble attract the butterflies themselves. Fringing some of these rides in the spring are the flowers, some pink some blue, of the rare narrow-leaved lungwort. A close relative is cultivated in cottage gardens under the name Joseph and Mary, a double name for the twin colours.

Wild columbines are most frequent on the chalk but they occur in a few places in the Forest. A small shrub, not more than two feet tall and bearing red berries, is the butcher's broom, a plant very tolerant of shade. On dry, sandy soil in fairly open situations whortleberry, sometimes called bilberry, may be found. This is a dwarf sub-shrub belonging to the heath family but with deciduous leaves. The rose-pink, urn-shaped flowers are not very conspicuous but are followed by blackberries which make delicious tarts. They are still gathered for this purpose from the moors of Northern England but there are few places in the Forest where they grow in sufficient profusion.

Although about 700 species of wild flower are thought to grow in the New Forest, nearly a third of the total on the British list, nothing like this number will be seen by the average visitor, and many are short-lived anyway due to animal grazing.

Wild lungwort grows in the Forest in March

The Roots of the Forest

Apart from the inclosures, the New Forest has to many people the appearance of a truly wild landscape, and they believe that they are looking at natural woodland. But appearances can be deceptive. The truth is that at least from Norman times and probably well before, the Forest has been carefully 'managed' in the interests both of hunting and the keeping of domestic animals. A tree-lover arriving in the New Forest for the first time will be as much impressed by what he does not see as by what is visible. He will soon notice the absence or rarity of certain trees and shrubs such as ash, elm, lime, hazel and maple, most of which occur commonly outside the Forest boundaries.

The common trees can be divided into two groups in a rough classification; those which are commercially grown in the inclosures, and those which seed themselves readily outside. There are a few – oak, beech and Scots pine – which appear in both groups.

If one were asked to select just one particular species as representative of the Forest it would without question have to be the oak for several reasons. It is both widespread and numerous; it holds an honoured place in maritime history; and last but not least, it has been the premier forest tree for centuries and has religious associations. Many shapely old oaks can still be seen in the Forest, especially in those open woods which have been classified as Ancient and Ornamental. Many of these oaks have been pollarded, that is, their tops were cut when they were young trees to provide winter food for the deer which were an all-important feature of the Forest and a prime reason for its existence. When, in the 18th century, the growing of greatly-increased numbers of oak to build the wooden ships of the Navy became urgent, pollarding was stopped by parliament as a pollarded tree produced inferior timber.

Walkers amid the Douglas fir at Bolderwood

It has been estimated that nearly 300 species of animal, mainly invertebrates, are found only on oak, whilst another 1,200 feed on oak as well as other foods. There are two native kinds of oak which grow in the Forest. Much the commonest is the pedunculate oak, which has almost stemless leaves but stalked acorns, whilst in the other kind, the sessile oak, the position is reversed; it has stalked leaves but sessile acorns.

Several of the most beautiful woods, for example Ridley, Mark Ash, Soarley Beeches and Berry Beeches, consist principally of beech. This lovely tree has smooth grey bark and glossy green leaves. It is especially beautiful at two seasons – in the spring when the new leaves are soft and silky before the dust of summer has settled on them, and again in the autumn when their colour changes first to gold and eventually to a rich brown. Many of them have been pollarded like the oaks and this enhances their beauty in old age. Beech will tolerate shade but it is also a light excluder so that few wild flowers will be seen growing beneath it. There is however, a very distinctive moss known as the white fork-moss whose cushions, greyish white in a dry season, are often abundant under beech.

The birch is a slender, graceful tree well distributed in the inclosures and on the heaths, especially on light soils. It is sometimes called the Queen of the woods. Two native species grow in the Forest. The silver birch has pendulous branches and white bark, and grows on dry soils. The downy birch is found in wet situations, is upright in growth and the leaves have soft hairs. In some birches you will see clusters of twigs somewhat resembling bird nests. These are 'witches' brooms' and are a deformity caused by the activity of gall mite. The large, greyish white fungus seen high up on some trunks is a bracket fungus which was once used for the manufacture of razor-strops.

Holly trees are common enough in the open Forest. The male and female flowers grow on separate trees, and the berries which follow are eaten by birds, especially the visiting Scandinavian thrushes. Holly produces a hard, white wood which is difficult to work but is used for inlaying and by cabinet makers.

Scots pine is numerous on the heaths but it is not native to the Forest. The first experimental

The pedunculate oak can live 800 years or more

plantings were of a small number at Ocknell and Bolderwood in 1776. They successfully proved the species' viability, now shown by the way it sows itself so freely. The name which the foresters give for the self-propagation of a non-native species is 'sub-spontaneous'.

Other trees growing outside the inclosures, chiefly in small numbers, are yew, whitebeam, rowan and crab apple on the heaths, whilst alders flourish alongside the streams.

In the inclosures a broadleaved species which has been planted is the sweet chestnut, which requires a sandy soil. In the autumn when the nuts fall, parties of grey squirrels can be heard noisily squabbling over the feast. The timber is similar to oak and is used for paling.

Larches are unusual in that although they are conifers they lose their leaves in winter. The vivid green needles of a stand of larch are very attractive in early spring. Like sweet chestnut it does best on light soils. The common European species was first introduced to Britain by the Duke of Atholl in the 17th century. In the 19th century the Japanese larch was brought in and planted amongst other places at Dunkeld, where at the beginning of this century a vigorous hybrid between the two species was discovered. All three species have been planted in the New Forest. The wood is used for a variety of purposes including poles, pit props, railway sleepers and fencing.

Scots pine is common in the Forest

One conifer which does exceptionally well in the Forest is Douglas fir, the tallest being over 150 feet tall. Its Latin name – *pseudotsuga menziesii* honours a Scotsman called Archibald Menzies, a surgeon and naturalist who in the late 18th century discovered the species in western North America. David Douglas, a young gardener who, working under the auspices of the Royal Horticultural Society, sent back seed to Britain in 1827, is remembered by the common name. Its coarse-textured timber is often known as Oregon pine and it is used for a variety of purposes.

Of the true pines, Scots and Corsican are frequently grown, the latter lacking the red-brown bark of Scots pine. Other common conifers include the Norway spruce which provide the traditional Christmas trees, Sitka spruce with stiff needles, western hemlock, western red cedar and giant silver fir, the last being one of the fastest-growing conifers.

Silver birch in autumn

A Sika stag and hinds amongst the silver birch

The Forest Family Tree

Take a look at this ancient oak. With its short, stout trunk and picturesque circle of branches it is one of the glories of the Forest. As well as arousing our admiration it excites our curiosity. What is the story of its life? Beyond any doubt, it, and others like it, have had a fascinating history.

It was the year 1782. George III was on the throne, the Marquis of Rockingham was Prime Minister and the United States had just declared itself independent of Britain. But in the New Forest humbler things were happening, though significant enough in their own way.

In the autumn of that year a jay could be seen making periodic flights to and from a large oak. Closer inspection would have revealed that it was raiding the tree for acorns which it was then carrying to various makeshift larders in the ground. It was wisely storing up food reserves for a possible severe winter ahead. Several acorns were taken to a small cache under a holly bush and subsequently forgotten. A long-tailed field mouse soon discovered the store and consumed most of it until he was disturbed.

The remaining three acorns successfully germinated and each produced its initial pair of leaves known as cotyledons, but these two seedlings were quickly eaten by rabbits. The third miraculously survived. It continued to send down into the soil the thin wisp which would eventually become the giant tap root so characteristic of the oak. The tiny seedling now and for the next few years was at its most vulnerable stage. The dangers were many. The commoners' animals and the deer browse at will across the Forest, a roe buck might well choose it as a territorial marking post and fray the sapling, or a hungry vole might ring bark it at the base, not to mention the risk of fire. There was, however, a powerful point in the young tree's favour; it was protected by the spiny leaves of the holly. Due to this it survived and prospered.

The acorns of the pendunculate oak fall in October

Ten years after germination the young tree produced its first few flowers, much earlier than if it had been growing in a plantation. Then in 1805, the year of the Battle of Trafalgar, a passing keeper out looking for winter food for the deer chanced upon it and lopped the main stem at a height of six feet above ground. He did not seem to know or care that over a hundred years previously an Act of 1698 had made his action illegal. His motive in any case was not entirely altruistic. After the deer had stripped the bark he intended to sell the branches for firewood and make a little extra money on the side as custom used to permit.

Resenting this attack upon its trunk the young oak reacted by sending out several vigorous branches to replace the lost stem. It was now a pollarded oak.

A tree is one of Nature's factories. Let us imagine that we can look at a cross-section of the trunk. Our eyes are immediately drawn to the concentric circles which are called annular rings, each of which represents a year's growth. Counting the rings will reveal the tree's age. The width of the individual rings varies according to the growing conditions in a particular year.

Closer inspection of the cross-section shows other features. Beginning from the outside we at once recognise the bark. This is like an overcoat and performs a valuable function in protecting the internal cells from damage and also in preventing excess evaporation. The next layer is known as bast or phloem and its purpose is to convey and

A germinating acorn in autumn

distribute the organic products manufactured by the leaves downwards to the trunk and roots. Continuing inwards we come to the cambium which is the growing point of the new wood. This divides into two, part forming new phloem and part extending the sapwood, thus making another annular ring. The function of the sapwood is to transport nutrients upwards. So the trunk is a kind of Jacob's ladder, only with particles instead of angels ascending and descending. Finally, in the centre is the heartwood or pith, which is darker and harder than the sapwood.

Whilst the roots themselves serve the dual purpose of anchoring the tree and acting as a food reservoir, the delicate hairs attached to the roots have been designed for the absorption of water and minerals from the soil.

The tens of thousands of leaves which adorn the upper part of the tree, technically termed the crown, form what has been called a starch factory. They serve a three-fold purpose, enabling the oak to breathe, to expel excess water, and by a complicated

A pendunculate oak in autumn

process known as photosynthesis to manufacture first the sugar, then the starch by which the tree lives.

By late autumn the oak has discarded its leaves. This is an adjustment to the climatic conditions and enables the tree to reach a resting phase. So each year chemical changes take place in the leaves causing them to turn brown and fall.

But we must return to our oak's life story. It is early summer in 1812. The bark, which up to now has been a smooth-textured grey, is beginning to darken and small furrows are starting to appear. In a few month's time Napoleon will be shivering in the snow on the way to Moscow and here in the Forest a forester is busy selecting trees to make the ships to win the war against the French, not knowing that the decisive battle would be fought not at sea but on land in three years' time at Waterloo. His route home leads him past our tree and he cannot resist giving an appraising glance, though he knows that it probably will not be ready for felling before another

The young oak seedling

ninety years and philosophically accepts that he will not be around when it happens.

Each spring the oak blooms. The male flowers are yellowish catkins and the female flowers are an inconspicuous brown, borne on a long stalk. The invisible pollen from the catkins is distributed by the wind and in extreme cases may be carried more than ten miles. The acorns, on the other hand, drop within a few yards of the tree where they will germinate if allowed to do so. The acorn crop of our tree over the years has been eaten by a miscellany of creatures including domestic animals, deer, grey squirrels, badgers, mice and birds.

If many animals gather beneath its shade, more, far more, live amongst its branches. Beetle larvae honeycomb the bark and many other invertebrates live in the crevices until eaten by the trunk-climbing birds. Many birds continue to perch among the branches. Purple hairstreak butterflies flutter in the sunshine, followed each night by innumerable moths. Insects galore live in and on the leaves and a most spectacular effect was produced in 1980 by the larvae of the green oak roller moth which almost denuded the tree of its leaves.

What changes this old oak has known in its lifetime! It has witnessed the reign of nine monarchs, lived through a number of wars and seen transport develop from the horse to Concorde, from sailing ships to nuclear-powered submarines.

Now, past its prime, it proudly celebrates its double centenary. Take a last, long, lingering look at the moss-festooned trunk, the shapely branches dotted with polypody ferns, the twigs be-medalled with marble galls, for when it and its pollarded fellows finally die and perhaps disappear from the Forest we may never see their like again. The foresters of today have begun to repollard some younger oak trees in order to perpetuate this ancient system of aboriculture. The trees when treated will last much longer than a maiden tree!

The Forest as a Factory

Hardly any woods exist in Britain today which can accurately be described as 'natural' in the fullest sense of that word. Certainly, they do not exist in the New Forest, which has been managed by man for many centuries. At first this was necessary primarily for the deer, as befits a Royal Chase, but also from early days for the benefit of the domestic animals of the local inhabitants.

In Tudor times a slight but significant change occurred as coppices appeared and timber was regarded in a new light as an economic crop. As the years went by this approach gathered momentum particularly when the large, wooden men-of-war came to be built. When these were replaced by ironclads other timber uses materialised – poles for various purposes, pit props, fencing, gate posts, railway sleepers, and pulp wood for paper manufacture.

One vitally important fact which is often not realised by the casual visitor to the countryside is that vegetation is not static but dynamic; it is constantly responding to changes in climate, soil conditions and insect populations. Therefore if it is to serve the interests and needs of humans it must be managed. In olden time the sovereign gave the New Forest his direct personal attention, successively replaced in later years by various crown organisations. It was not until 1919 that the Forest Commission was formed, out of a natural need for a forestry authority.

So the duty of the Forestry Commission in the Forest is just to supervise the growing of trees? Any suggestion to this effect would probably be greeted with hollow laughter by the officials of that body.

For the fact is that the Forest has been a mass of conflicting interests for some considerable time and as the years roll by, more new interests emerge, each with its own point of view, to stake a claim in the country's playground. The commoners and their jealously-guarded rights, hunting, shooting and fishing interests, horse-riders, conservationists, naturalists with various concerns, campers and caravanners, artists, ramblers, orienteers, model boat owners are all, in one way or another, the responsibility of the Forestry Commission. Since many of these activities are at variance with each other the Commission has to try and maintain a balance, or at least an uneasy peace between them.

Additionally, the Commission is required to run a forestry business, as far as possible on an economic basis. There are two broad classes of woodlands in the New Forest – the semi-natural woods which are defined in the 1877 Act as Ancient and Ornamental, and the inclosures which contain the planted trees.

The 1877 Act forbade any enclosing of the Ancient and Ornamental woods and the foresters had no power to touch them. But woodlands cannot be left to their own devices. What happened was that each year a number of trees fell, but since these woods were wide open to cattle, ponies and deer, natural regeneration virtually ceased. If this situation was not remedied the result in the long term would be at best a considerable reduction in area and at worst, the disappearance of these magnificent woods. This view is not shared by everyone, not even every arboriculturalist, but we have only to look at the woods bereft of seedlings to see the contrast with the prolific regeneration within the small enclosed areas. These regeneration inclosures were authorised by an Act of 1949 and extended by a further act in 1964. The fences are only temporary and will be removed when the young trees have grown beyond the stage when they would sustain serious damage.

The main inclosures used to have a distinctive type of fencing with strap-like bands instead of wire but this tradition has died out for economic reasons.

An 118 year-old stand of Douglas fir at Bolderwood

California Big Tree at Rhinefield

Neither type presents much of an obstacle to the deer who go under and over them. From the last century onwards conifers have increasingly come to predominate although considerable areas of deciduous plantings exist, some in mixed stands. The reason for the preference for conifers is that they are more suited to the less fertile soils of the later inclosures; they are better fitted for today's market requirements and, most important, they come much earlier to maturity.

Aesthetic objections are often raised against alien conifers. Certainly the serried ranks of any species grown under the monocultural, even-aged method can be far from attractive in their early stages but there are plenty of places where, except to a purist, mature conifers are aesthetically satisfying. Various cameos flit across the memory – the splendid conifers flanking the Ornamental Drive; a clump of pines on the skyline; a group of larches whose vivid green needles lighten the sombreness of nearby oaks; a V-shaped phalanx of spruce under snow creating a fairyland of delight; the vast rolling sweep of Highland Water inclosure – but in the end, 'beauty is in the eye of the beholder'. As a goodwill gesture the Forestry Commission has designated certain inclosures amounting to 1,100 acres as amenity woods where scenic values have special consideration.

Where an area has been felled there is a choice of either replanting with seedlings or relying on natural regeneration. The latter is increasingly favoured where this is possible. In this case, a number of good quality mature trees, evenly spaced out, are left to act as 'mother' trees.

Where, however, replanting is indicated, the seedlings are obtained from the Forest's own nurseries. The tiny trees are planted very close together. In order to harvest 250 mature trees per hectare about 3,000 seedlings per hectare would be planted. For some years the wild flowers, birds and insects remain those of an open ground habitat but as the trees grow and light is excluded the flora and fauna become much diminished. Knots disfigure wood and since they originate from branches these are lopped off at an early age in a process known as brashing. Gradually over the years selective thinnings take place as the less desirable trees are eliminated leaving relatively few good quality trees as the final crop. The wheel has then turned full circle and the process is ready to begin all over again.

The New Forest from a forester's point of view has had its successes and its failures. The successes include fast growth of Douglas fir, Corsican pine and the natural regeneration of all trees planted since 1700. Failures might include the vast areas lost by fire from incendiary bombs in World War II and the death of so many beech trees in the 1975–76 drought. We can rest assured that the future of this ancient forest is a very real concern for the forester and he will continue to endure the pressures of the future and still grow and manage his trees.

Wild cherry at Roe

Beech in the Ancient and Ornamental Woodland

Making Friends with the Forest

Today's visitors to the New Forest do not come to hunt the deer or to pursue self-indulgent pleasures like the lords of centuries past. They come, usually part of a family unit, to enjoy the Forest in a passive way, perhaps to seek a moment of tranquillity away from modern day pressures, and with an altruistic concern for those who follow. They are aware that the Forest's special beauty is a result of the gradual process of change which has altered its function over the years from hunting ground to timber inclosure, culminating in the 1877 New Forest Act which paid special attention to the maintenance of its 'picturesque character'. This has been achieved, in spite of the fairly recent arrival of railway, road, industry and housing springing up around the Forest and encroaching on its boundaries.

To ensure that the New Forest remains a sanctuary where wildlife can be seen in its natural surroundings and the secrets of the countryside, though observed, go undisturbed, a rigid kind of 'country code' is necessary, and must be honoured by everyone who visits the Forest in order for it to survive for another 900 years or more. Many of the rules have been made for the well-being of the visitor, as in many parts the Forest is as wild and untamed as anywhere they are likely to find themselves. A large variety of rare wild flowers grows in the Forest, but the temptation to pick or dig up these beautiful things has to be resisted in order that other visitors can enjoy them.

A favourite area with campers, the Forest has been provided by the Forestry Commission with certain designated sites for camping and caravanning. The standard of facilities at these sites varies, but they are all very popular, and as camping is allowed nowhere else in the Forest but at these sites it is wise to check in advance with the Forestry Commission if accommodation is available, especially in the height of summer. Always keep valuable possessions locked away either in the car or caravan, and keep dogs on a lead at all times – they must not be allowed to run wild and interfere with the animals.

Some of the designated car parks, of which there are 140, are equipped with picnic facilities such as tables and litter bins. Picnic or camp fires are not permitted, nor are stoves of any kind, and smoking in the Forest is discouraged because of the huge risk of fire. Special barbecue hearths can be reserved by application to the Forestry Commission at Lyndhurst. The Forestry Commission clears approximately 1,000 tons of litter from the Forest each year, and the careless shedding of a tin can or a polythene bag not only spoils the look of the Forest, it can endanger the animals. Feeding the animals is an offence and carries a £20 fine. Ponies that have been fed stray on to the roads in search of more food from visitors, often resulting in car accidents.

Gladiolus

Marsh Gentian

Bog Orchid

Remember that the animals have right of way; in fact, due to their tendency to wander at will many commoners choose to fence their gardens with high, prickly hedges in order to discourage inquisitive ponies from grazing on their flower beds. The inclosures are fenced and gated to prevent ponies and cattle from damaging rare trees and plants. Forest walkers must remember one golden rule – gates must be shut behind you.

Although a series of Forest walks is described in the atlas section of this publication, the temptation is to set off on an uncharted tour of the Forest without first mapping out a route. This is not to be recommended; it is surprisingly easy to get lost in a forest of this size. The atlas in this book makes an ideal basis for

Pony and Dartford Warbler

planning an excursion. Remember to take a good look at your starting point before setting off – it might look very different from another angle! Be observant as you walk and try to notice unusual features along your path – they will help you if you need to retrace your steps. A 'Silva' type compass is always useful, and, if you are planning a long walk, some warm clothes (it can turn chilly in the evenings), a simple picnic (pubs and restaurants are few and far between) and a torch would keep you going in an emergency. Stout walking boots or wellingtons are advisable all the year round due to marshy soil and the notorious New Forest bogs.

Always supervise children who may wish to swim or paddle in the Forest's many rivers and streams. Some of these, as a result of winter flood, have sudden deep and dangerous holes in the river floor.

The only poisonous reptile to look out for is the adder, recognised by its 'V' marked back. They are usually found dozing in the sun in the heathland and will only attack if they feel threatened. If you are bitten by a snake the drill is: keep calm, wash area with clean water, do not cut, burn or attempt to suck the poison out of the wound. Call a doctor or go at once to Southampton or Lyndhurst hospitals. They stock anti-snake bite serum.

Adder

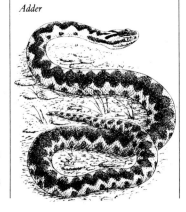

Where to go...What to see...Where to stay...What to do...

The River Avon undulates through the counties of Hampshire and Dorset, creating the boundary between them for much of its length

Aldridge Hill Campsite, Hampshire

Map Ref: 10SU2803

A small informal campsite reached by Forest track off the Rhinefield Ornamental Drive, 1 mile west of Brockenhurst. Campers are expected to provide their own toilets. Tickets can be obtained from the warden on arrival or first thing the following morning. The camp is close to Ober Water and the Forest walks of the Rhinefield Ornamental Drive, Poundhill Inclosure and Vinney Ridge as well as the more open aspect of Ober Heath.

Ashurst, Hampshire

Map Ref: 7SU3310

On the A35 Southampton–Lyndhurst road, 2 miles south-west of Totton, Ashurst is easily overlooked. From the road this village appears to be a linear collection of attractive houses and a small parade of shops brought to an abrupt halt by a railway bridge on the main Southampton–Bournemouth line. In fact this village and its leafy neighbour, Woodlands, are prime residential areas for commuters to the industrial and commercial centre of Southampton only 7 miles away. The railway bridge marks the boundary of the New Forest. At Ashurst Lodge, now a private house, in woodland 1 mile south of the village, are remains of an Elizabethan industrial site where saltpetre (potassium nitrate – a constituent of gunpowder as well as a meat preservative) was produced for a short while until the area was discovered to be uneconomic to mine.

South-west of the village is the Forestry Commission's 280-pitch campsite set in Ashurst Woods. The site has toilets, hot water and showers and includes facilities for the disabled.

The site is a good base for the exploration of both the northern and eastern edge of the Forest and there are many opportunities for walks in the northern valley of the Beaulieu River which can be fished with permits from the site information office. No dogs are allowed on the site.

AA recommends:
Hotels: Busketts Lawn, Woodlands, 2-star, *tel.* Ashurst 2272
Woodlands Lodge, Woodlands, 2-star, *tel.* Ashurst 2257
Campsite: Ashurst Camp, Ashurst Woods. 2-pennants, *tel.* Cadnam 3494
Self-catering: Foxhills Cottage, Ashurst *tel.* Ashurst 2309
Merrie Downs, Woodlands *tel.* Ashurst 2830

The River Avon

Rising in the Vale of Pewsey (Wiltshire) Hampshire's Avon flows directly south across Salisbury Plain, its upper reaches being the classic trout-fishing chalk stream. South of Salisbury, where it is joined by the major tributaries Bourne, Wylye and Nadder, the waters assume a slower character and, while the river still enjoys a considerable salmon run, coarse fish are the predominant species. From Breamore south through Fordingbridge and Ringwood to its joint estuary with the Dorset Stour at Christchurch, the Avon's valley marks the western boundary of the New Forest, and for much of its length the river itself is the Hampshire/Dorset county boundary. The river is tidal for only one mile north of its confluence with the Stour. As the river crosses an area of considerable prehistoric, Roman and medieval interest there are many ancient ford and bridge points along its length. Fordingbridge's name is directly derived from its importance as an Avon crossing and other traces of the river's significance can be found at

Bickton, Ibsley, Avon Tyrrell and Christchurch itself where both the river mouth and the crossing were guarded by an ancient castle. Today the river is most remembered for its excellent coarse fishing sport, especially the barbel, chub and roach of the Royalty Fisheries which extend for one mile from Alberbush to Christchurch Town Bridge. Although catches have declined over the last 10 years, intensive management and rehabilitation of the waters by the Wessex Water Authority shows signs of reversing the trend.

Balmer Lawn, Hampshire

Map Ref: 10SU3003

Bounded by the Lymington River to the south, Balmer Lawn is about 200 acres of open heath and grass lying between Hollands Wood and the Pignal Inclosure woodlands on the fringe of Brockenhurst. Scattered trees punctuate this open space which is criss-crossed by paths and the tracks of grazing horses and cattle which keep the vegetation under close control. Balmer Lawn was once the site of a race-course around which New Forest ponies were spurred to boost the fortunes of their owners and spectators. The riverside here is a popular picnic spot with a good car park – the river is an inviting place to cool off on a hot day. In its quieter reaches near Balmer Lawn the Lymington River is fishable for native brown trout, on tickets to be obtained from the Forestry Commission information point in Lyndhurst's main car park. During the summer, horse-drawn wagon rides are available through the Inclosures from Balmer Lawn.

AA recommends:
Hotels: Ladbroke Balmer Lawn Hotel, Lyndhurst Road, Brockenhurst, 3-star, *tel.* Lymington 23116

Bashley, Hampshire

See key map

A quiet village on the fringes of the New Forest which has only become well-known since the opening of a large holiday complex at Bashley Park. Although fully booked in summer, little activity is apparent from the B3055 which goes past the Park's gates, since the campsite and chalets are positioned well back among woodland in the grounds. With a swimming pool, bars, restaurants, shop and games on tap, few holidaymakers need to go outside Bashley Park's portals, although the shops and Arnewood Sports Centre at New Milton are just along the road, as is the beach at Barton on Sea. Nearby Walkford Brook, which wends its way south through the Forest to emerge through a natural chine called Chewton Bunny into the Solent was used extensively for smuggling in the 19th century; today it is more widely called Chewton Glen, and famous for a top class hotel and restaurant.

AA recommends:
Hotels: Chewton Glen, Christchurch Road, Red Star, Country House Hotel, 1-rosette, 4-star, *tel.* Highcliffe 5341
Garages: Coopers, Fernhill Lane, 1-spanner, *tel.* New Milton 612121
Campsites: Bashley Park, 4-pennants, *tel.* New Milton 612340
Self-catering: as above

Beaulieu, Hampshire

Map Ref: 11SU3802

At the junction of the B3054 and B3056 and at the tidal limit of the Beaulieu River stands Beaulieu itself, an entertainments park of buildings ancient and modern. The principal building is now the Palace House, the home of Lord Montagu, whose family has lived here since 1538. The House is open to the public and contains a considerable collection of paintings and furnishings. But this was only the gatehouse to Beaulieu Abbey, founded in 1204 by King John as a monastery of the Cistercian order. The Abbey was

destroyed during the Reformation and, today, only the refectory remains wholly standing, converted into a distinctive parish church. Ruined parts of the Abbey visible include the cloisters, part of the chapter house and a section of the monks' dormitory. To many Beaulieu visitors, however, the history is secondary in attraction. For Beaulieu is the home of the National Motor Museum, one of the world's largest collections of vehicles and motoring memorabilia displayed in a setting designed by Sir Hugh Casson. The grounds can be toured by a futuristic high-level monorail, by miniature trains and by a mock vintage bus. Children's playgrounds and numerous other family attractions are laid on throughout the year. The gardens of Palace House are notable and both wooded parts of the estate and some of the surrounding river valley countryside can be appreciated on the 2¼-mile waymarked trail to Buckler's Hard and its ancient shipyards.

AA recommends:
Hotels: Montagu Arms, 3-star, *tel.* Beaulieu 612324
Garages: The Garage, Lyndhurst Road, 2-spanners, *tel.* Beaulieu 612444
Self-catering: Culverley Old Farm Cottage, *tel.* Beaulieu 612260

Beaulieu Heath

Map Ref: 11SU3500

One of the largest expanses of open ground in the Forest, Beaulieu Heath lies to the west of East Boldre village and is bisected by the B3054 Beaulieu–Lymington Road. Covering some five square miles, the heath is part grass and marsh but it is predominantly heather-covered. The main grass areas are those of the old Beaulieu Airfield, a wartime flying base that continued in use until 1959. There is considerable evidence to show that it was an area in which the population flourished from prehistoric to medieval times. The heath is dotted with many tumuli (prehistoric burial places), there is a defensive earthwork rampart straddling

Portraits in Beaulieu Palace House

the B3055 at the northern edge of the open space and the clear patterns of a medieval field system are visible close to Crockford Clump, one of the best examples of this type of remains to be found in the Forest. Hatchet Pond is an ancient artificial water which probably fed a mill in nearby East Boldre. Today it has been stocked with coarse fish and tickets to enjoy some sport here can be obtained from Forestry Commission offices. The paths of the Lady Cross Walk lace across the heath which is provided with a number of car parks. From higher points of the area there are distant views across the Solent to the Isle of Wight and there are picnic areas at most of the designated car parks.

Beaulieu Road Station, Hampshire

Map Ref: 7SU3406

A railway halt on the Southampton–Brockenhurst–Bournemouth line, Beaulieu Road Station serves only the nearby Beaulieu Road Hotel public house for most of the year. But on five occasions in the New Forest calendar

---

The Beaulieu Estate

The Maritime Museum at Buckler's Hard, on Lord Montagu's estate, is a treasure house of fascinating souvenirs celebrating the New Forest's long associations with Britain's maritime history. Opened in 1963 by the late Earl Mountbatten of Burma, the Museum contains clever scale models, relics and literature about the village, the Forest and the sea. There is a replica of the *Agamemnon*, reputed to be Nelson's favourite battleship. Another model shows the village nearly 200 years ago when it was a thriving shipbuilding centre. HMS *Swiftsure* is under construction and alongside HMS *Euryalus* waits on the stocks ready for launching. Nearby are the timber yards, slipways and workers' cottages, including the home of master shipbuilder Henry Adams, now a hotel.

Buckler's Hard and the Beaulieu River also played host to round-the-world mariner Sir Francis Chichester – the Museum documents his sailing adventures and successes, for it was from here that he set out in his yacht, *Gypsy Moth III*, on several transatlantic races. *Gypsy Moth IV*, in which he sailed single-handed around the world, is still moored in the Beaulieu River.

Beautiful gardens surround the Palace House at Beaulieu

this lonely spot on the B3056 Lyndhurst–Beaulieu road becomes the focus of horse-lovers' attentions. For this is the site of the April, August, September, October and November New Forest Pony Sales, events which are held in an almost fair-like atmosphere and which attract a wide cross-section of potential buyers from Romany traders to children looking for their first mount. Traditionally the foals, predominantly colts, are sold in the morning, starting with the better-bred ponies eligible for registration with the New Forest Pony Breeding and Cattle Society, followed by those that are already registered and, finally, the poorly bred horses ineligible for registry. Other horses and adult ponies from the area are sold during the afternoon.

Boldre, Hampshire

Map Ref: 10 SZ 3198

Straddling the Lymington River 2 miles north of Lymington itself, Boldre is a small edge-of-the-Forest village. The remote 13th-century church of St John contains many items of interest including a huge iron key said to have been for a door to Beaulieu Abbey. The poet Robert Southey is recorded as having married here, there is a memorial service each May to the dead sailors of HMS *Hood* killed in battle against the *Bismarck* in 1941 and an exquisite modern stained-glass window. In School Lane, a house called Spinners has beautiful gardens landscaped and maintained by the owners. Azaleas, rhododendrons, camellias and magnolias are interplanted with primulas, blue poppies and other woodland and ground cover plants many of which can be bought here (open Easter – mid July, 2pm–7pm, not Mondays).

Beaulieu's National Motor Museum is a well-known crowd puller for the mechanically-minded. Footsore visitors are transported back in time on a vintage bus, or into the future on a space-age monorail

Bournemouth, Dorset

See key map

Until the early 19th century Bournemouth was only a small hamlet set in the valley of a stream called The Bourne. Surrounding the valley were heathland and pine woods – the local industries were fishing and smuggling. It was the Georgians who discovered Bournemouth's mild climate and bracing atmosphere; the two ideal

facets of a potential resort. The town's expansion dates back to around 1810, but it was the Victorians who laid down much of the stately, garden resort that still attracts many thousands of holidaymakers to its seven miles of sands and its spectacular 100ft cliffs. At the town's heart is the valley floor, landscaped to form the attractive Upper and Lower Bourne Gardens, while to east and west of the pier which marks the Bourne's actual mouth, the cliffs are topped by the imposing façades of hotels and the summer homes of the Victorian and Edwardian rich. At intervals the cliffs are split by steep tree-lined valleys known as chines, many of them landscaped and traversed by walks down to the promenade which can also be reached by two cliff lifts and a zigzag cliff path. Much open heathland has been preserved within the town limits, several areas of both Bournemouth and neighbouring Parkstone having been laid out as golf courses of a very high standard. Both Queen's Park (a championship course) and Meyrick Park are municipal parkland courses. Bournemouth is host to county class cricket and major tennis tournaments.

As a first-class holiday resort, Bournemouth offers a wide range of entertainments throughout the year with many annual summer attractions. In the pier area of the promenade are the kind of amusements associated with brasher resorts, but the town is better known for the regular recitals of its Symphony Orchestra, visiting opera companies and star performer variety shows. Ice shows at the resort's rink and an Aqua Show at the Pier Approach Baths are summer crowd-pullers. Just as popular are tours of the town on open-topped double-decker buses, an ideal way to appreciate Bournemouth's geography. The town has some fascinating museum

Part of Bournemouth's attractions – the gardens at Boscombe Chine

collections. The Big Four Railway Museum, for example, has static and working model displays of steam memorabilia, the Rothesay Museum houses a unique collection of typewriters and the Russell-Cotes Art Gallery & Museum has a room dedicated to the great actor Sir Henry Irving. Bournemouth's other associations with the famous include the site of the house in which Robert Louis Stevenson wrote both the last chapters of *Kidnapped* and *Dr Jekyll and Mr Hyde*, and the town's appearance as 'Sandbourne' in Thomas Hardy's *Tess of the D'Urbervilles*. Bournemouth is a major transport centre with good connections by train to London (Waterloo) and the West Country and an international airport (Hurn) with regular flights to France and the Channel Islands.

The ruins of St Leonard's Chapel, Buckler's Hard

AA recommends:
Hotels: Carlton, East Cliff, 5-star, *tel.* Bournemouth 22011
Royal Bath, Bath Road, 5-star, *tel.* Bournemouth 25555
East Cliff Court, East Overcliff Drive, 4-star, *tel.* Bournemouth 24545
Highcliff, West Cliff, St Michael's Road, 4-star, *tel.* Bournemouth 27702
Marsham Court, Russell Cotes Road, 4-star, *tel.* Bournemouth 22111
Palace Court, Westover Road, 4-star, *tel.* Bournemouth 27681
Anglo-Swiss, Gervis Road, East Cliff, 3-star, *tel.* Bournemouth 24794
Angus, Bath Road, 3-star, *tel.* Bournemouth 26420
Broughty Ferry Children's Hotel, Sea Road, Boscombe, 3-star, *tel.* Bournemouth 35333
Burley Court, Bath Road, 3-star, *tel.* Bournemouth 22824
Cecil, Parsonage Road, Bath Hill, 3-star,

Several large department stores and arcades full of specialist shops make Bournemouth a shopper's paradise

Smuggling

The New Forest was no different from any other part of the country in the early half of the 19th century. Smuggling was rife because of exorbitant food prices and swingeing taxes, and it was not only practised by gangs of criminals and small-time rogues. Whole families, even doctors and clerics, became involved in what was euphemistically called 'free trading'. But of course, those who took the greatest risks – and rewards – were those who sailed across the Channel to France and returned under cover of darkness to land their contraband of tea, brandy and tobacco in the coves along the coast.

Hampshire's seashore lends itself to smuggling as there are many natural creeks and inlets extending far inland to the leafy cover of the Forest itself. The most popular smugglers' routes were along the glen at Chewton Bunny near New Milton, and the Boldre and Beaulieu rivers. Once in the Forest the kegs and sacks were divided up for onward transportation to towns such as Salisbury, Ringwood and Southampton. The thatched Cat and Fiddle pub at Hinton was one of these distribution centres; today it is an extremely popular stopping place for thirsty travellers on the A35. Another smugglers' pub was the Queen's Head at Burley, these days better known as the local hunt's meeting place in the hunting season.

To counteract smuggling, Customs and Excise appointed Riding Officers to chase offenders on land, and Revenue Cutters to intercept contraband at sea, but neither force was very successful. For the Cutters were too sluggish to catch the smugglers' boats and on land the communities were organised, in their own interests, to keep watch for the Riding Officers and warn their smuggling cohorts.

tel. Bournemouth 293336
Chesterwood, East Overcliff Drive, 3-star,
tel. Bournemouth 28057
Chine, Boscombe Spa Road, Boscombe,
3-star, tel. Bournemouth 36234
Cliff End, Manor Road, East Cliff, 3-star,
tel. Bournemouth 309711
Cliffside, East Overcliff Drive, 3-star,
tel. Bournemouth 25724
Hotel Courtlands, 16 Boscombe Spa Road,
East Cliff, 3-star, tel. Bournemouth 33070
Crest, Lansdowne, 3-star, White star hotel,
tel. Bournemouth 23262
Durley Dean, West Cliff Road, 3-star,
tel. Bournemouth 27711
Durley Hall, Durley Chine Road, 3-star,
tel. Bournemouth 766886
Durleston Court, Gervis Road, East Cliff,
3-star, tel. Bournemouth 291488
East Anglia, 6 Poole Road, 3-star,
tel. Bournemouth 765163
Embassy, Meyrick Road, 3-star,
tel. Bournemouth 20751
Grosvenor, Bath Road, East Cliff, 3-star,
tel. Bournemouth 28858
Hazelwood, Christchurch Road, East Cliff,
3-star, tel. Bournemouth 21367
Heathlands, Grove Road, East Cliff, 3-star,
tel. Bournemouth 23336
Ladbroke Savoy, West Hill Road, West
Cliff, 3-star, tel. Bournemouth 294241
Melford Hall, St Peter's Road, 3-star,
tel. Bournemouth 21516
Miramar, Grove Road, 3-star,
tel. Bournemouth 26581
Norfolk, Richmond Hill, 3-star,
tel. Bournemouth 21521
Pavilion, Bath Road, 3-star,
tel. Bournemouth 291266
Queens, Meyrick Road, East Cliff, 3-star,
tel. Bournemouth 24415
Trouville, Priory Road, 3-star,
tel. Bournemouth 22262
Wessex, West Cliff Road, 3-star,
tel. Bournemouth 21911
White Hermitage, Exeter Road, 3-star,
tel. Bournemouth 27363
*Bournemouth has a wide selection of 2- and
1-star hotels and self-catering
accommodation*

Restaurants: Boote's, 31 Southbourne
Grove, 2-forks, tel. Bournemouth 421240
La Cappa, 127 Poole Road, 2-forks,
tel. Bournemouth 761317
La Taverna, Westover Road, 2-forks,
tel. Bournemouth 27681
Crust, The Square, 1-fork,
tel. Bournemouth 21430
Trattoria San Marco, 148 Holdenhurst
Road, 1-fork, tel. Bournemouth 21132
Ann's Pantry, 129 Belle Vue Road,
Southbourne, tel. Bournemouth 426178
Fortes, The Square, tel. Bournemouth
24916
La Fontaine, 141 Belle Vue Road,
Southbourne, tel. Bournemouth 420537
The Old England, 74 Poole Road,
Westbourne, tel. Bournemouth 766475
Planters, 514 Christchurch Road,
Boscombe, tel. Bournemouth 302228
The Salad Centre, Post Office Road,
tel. Bournemouth 21720
Trattoria Tosca, 12 Richmond Hill,
tel. Bournemouth 23034

Garages: George Hartwell, 27–49
Holdenhurst Road, 3-spanners,
tel. Bournemouth 26566
St Christophers, 1191–1201 Christchurch

Road, Boscombe East, 3-spanners,
tel. Bournemouth 424381
Auto Service, 33 Robert Louis Stevenson
Avenue, Westbourne, 3-spanners,
tel. Bournemouth 763344
F English, Poole Road, 3-spanners,
tel. Bournemouth 762442
Hendy-Lennox, 9/19 Palmerston Road,
Boscombe, 3-spanners, tel. Bournemouth
39331
Henlys (South West) 16–18 Poole Road,
3-spanners, tel. Bournemouth 766031
Iford Bridge Motor Co, 1374 Christchurch
Road, 3-spanners, tel. Christchurch 483779
Westover Patrick's Motors, Castle Lane,
3-spanners, tel. Bournemouth 510201
*Bournemouth also has 2- and 1-spanner
garages*

A record of times past – the Russell Cotes Museum in Bournemouth

Bramshaw, Hampshire

Map Ref: 3SU2615

Deep in leafy woodlands, with greens
and oak verges grazed by pigs and
donkeys as well as the New Forest
ponies, Bramshaw village is bordered
by several National Trust-owned and
administered commons which include
the green at the village heart. Plaitford
Common to the north and Cadnam
Common to the east are both pock-
marked with Bronze Age barrows,
earthwork banks and boundary
palisades. Nearby sights include the
highest point in the New Forest,
Piper's Wait, and the old forest of
Bramshaw Woods.

A regiment of luxury hotels line Bournemouth's sea front

Bramshaw Telegraph, Hampshire

Map Ref: 2SU2216

At a point near the junction of the B3078 and B3080 in the north of the Forest, a chain of semaphore signalling stations was established during the Napoleonic Wars. Even now called Bramshaw Telegraph, the high ground on which it stood is 416 ft above sea

Breamore House is a dignified Elizabethan manor

Bournemouth's Russell Cotes Museum perches high on a windswept cliff

level, one of the highest points in the Forest. The semaphore signalling chains were used to pinpoint enemy fleets approaching Britain's shore and relay the information both to the fleet headquarters in Portsmouth and to the Admiralty in London. It is probable that the Bramshaw station was used to transmit intelligence and orders from Portsmouth to naval detachments operating from West Country ports. There is a car park at the Telegraph handy for exploring Island Thorns Inclosure to the south.

Breamore, Hampshire

Map Ref: 1SU1517

Breamore (or *Bremmer* as it is pronounced), is an attractive village with an almost intact Saxon church, an Elizabethan manor and a turf maze. The church dates from about 1000 and many of its original features are still visible, such as a defaced Saxon rood with the Virgin Mary and St John over the south door, and an Anglo-Saxon incription in 6-inch-high lettering. Breamore House is open to visitors

between spring and autumn and contains fine collections of paintings, tapestries and furniture. Also of interest to country lovers is a Countryside and Carriage Museum in the grounds which, with the aid of relics and reconstructed workshops, traces the history of agricultural tools and machinery. It houses well-preserved examples of coaches and steam engines. The 'Mizmaze' which is cut into the chalk on the hillside nearby, is nearly 30yds in width and of

VIPs of the Forest

Probably the first thing a schoolchild learns about the New Forest is that King Rufus was killed here while hunting. Yet it was his father, William I, of 1066-and-all-that, who first reserved the New Forest land as a royal hunting ground in about 1079.

Other generations of royals shared William's fascination with the Forest. King John founded the abbey at Beaulieu in 1204, and later that century Eleanor, queen of Edward I, was frequently seen walking through the Forest, by the side of the upper stretches of the Lymington River, north of Brockenhurst. Her favourite spot was named Queen's Bower after her. Charles I was made a reluctant 'guest' of Cromwell's troops at Hurst Castle in 1648, and the Duke of Monmouth was similarly detained at the White Hart Inn, Ringwood, in 1685.

Bishop's Dyke, east of Brockenhurst, is said to have been secured for the church by the Bishop of Winchester in the Middle Ages after he had been promised he could keep as much land as he could crawl around on his hands and knees in one day. As Master Keeper at Bolderwood Lodge, John, Lord de la Warre, erected a three-sided stone pillar in memory of King Rufus' death. The following century, Warden William Sturges Bourne had the much-visited and defaced stone covered with an iron casing.

More recent – and familiar – VIPs have been Theodore Roosevelt, who took a lengthy stroll from Stoney Cross to Black Knowl, north of Brockenhurst, in June 1910, and Generals Eisenhower and Montgomery who based themselves nearby at the Balmer Lawn Hotel for part of World War II. The artist Augustus John lived and died in Fordingbridge, and others buried in the Forest include Sir Arthur Conan Doyle at Minstead; Coventry Patmore, poet, at Lymington, and Mrs Alice Hargreaves, née Liddell, friend of Lewis Carroll.

Exhibits in Breamore's Countryside and Carriage Museum

Holidaymakers at Brockenhurst

Elizabethan elegance inside Breamore House

Breamore Museum Wheelwright's Shop △

The Forest in War

Because of its proximity to the docks and defences of Southampton, the New Forest lay vulnerable to enemy warfare during World War II. Several buildings in the quiet green villages were damaged, among them All Saints' Church, Dibden, and ponies were killed by stray bombs, but the worst damage was inflicted by exploding shells which set the plantations alight and produced an unquenchable inferno which caused destruction for miles. But the Forest didn't take the punishment passively. Thanks to tracks of flat, open heath camouflaged by plantations, wartime airfields were laid at Stoney Cross Plain, Fritham, Beaulieu Heath and Holmsley, and men, arms and planes were stationed here for both defensive and attacking missions.

The largest strip, opened in 1942, was at Holmsley, where men and aircraft were amassed for the invasion of Europe in 1944. Much of the planning for this top secret manoeuvre took place at the Balmer Lawn Hotel, Brockenhurst, which Generals Eisenhower and Montgomery commandeered for their operational headquarters. At Stoney Cross Plain, Fritham and Beaulieu Heath, tarmacadamed strips were laid and the gorse uprooted so that deep anti-aircraft emplacements could be dug; this line of defence, aided by the strategically-placed observation post at Hurst Castle, helped to fend off flying bombs and invasion targets from across the Channel. And not least, the Forest provided many thousands of tons of wood. Some of it was used to build wooden mine-sweepers, or it was cut into whatever lengths were required by 26 sawmills in the New Forest, among them those at Ashurst, Anderwood and Hawkhill.

In addition to the RAF and British troops, the Navy and other nationalities are remembered in World Wars I and II. At Mogshade a simple oak cross erected in 1946 commemorates the presence of the 3rd Canadian Division, and a plaque in Boldre church remembers the men of HMS *Hood* who were killed in action against the German battleship *Bismarck* in 1941. Near Millersford Bridge, a restored fireplace marks the spot where buildings occupied by Portuguese troops once stood in the 1914–18 war.

Buckler's Hard produced about 70 ships for the Navy between 1745 and 1822, including the three most famous of Nelson's fleet, *Agamemnon*, *Swiftsure* and *Euryalus*. And in the 17th century, much of the Forest, the western area in particular, witnessed the bloody strife of Civil War in its allegiance to the Royalists and the Duke of Monmouth.

See the Forest by wagon ▽

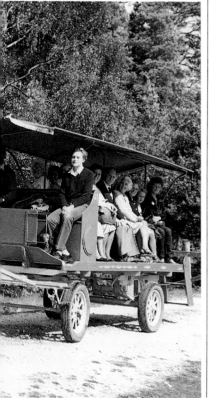

The Knightwood Oak – part of the Forest for 350 years

an intricate medieval Christian design. Its origins are uncertain, but one theory is that it was laid out by monks. To atone for a wrong-doing, it was usual, in those far-off days, to crawl round a maze on hands and knees as penance. To the west of Breamore is the charming village of Rockbourne with its restored Norman church and historic manor house. In 1942 archaeologists uncovered the remains of a large, 46-roomed Roman villa beneath the village cricket green. The foundations, open for public inspection, are intact with an intricate heating system, bath and fine mosaics. There is also a museum of other finds discovered during the excavation.

Brockenhurst, Hampshire

Map Ref: 10SU3002

Set amid some of the loveliest forestland, this picturesque village (the name means 'Badger's Wood') is much-visited in summer, yet retains a timeless peace. Ponies crop the village green without concern for the busy A337 from Lyndhurst, or the main London to Bournemouth railway line which crosses this busy road at a Continental-style level crossing. To the north of the village is a large Forestry Commission campsite at Hollands Wood, and Balmer Lawn with its stately hotel and broad sweep of turf where the Lymington River affords a chance to paddle and cool off in high summer. Harry 'Brusher' Mills, the Forest's official adder catcher, lived somewhere deep in the woods, but he was buried in the village churchyard; inside the church is a memorial to 101 New Zealanders who gave their lives in active service during World War I. Brockenhurst has a

number of riding stables in its area, for pony trekking on the open heath and Forest trails is popular; outstanding walks are at Ober Water Walks and to Queen Bower and the aptly-named Ornamental Drive with its large variety of specimen trees and flowering shrubs.

AA recommends:
Hotels: Carey's Manor, 3-star. *tel.* Lymington 22551
Forest Park Hotel, 3-star, *tel.* Lymington 22095
Ladbroke Balmer Lawn Hotel, 3-star, *tel.* Lymington 23116
Cloud Hotel, 2-star, *tel.* Lymington 22165
Watersplash Hotel, 2-star, *tel.* Lymington 22344
Garages: Gates Engineering, 3-spanners, *tel.* Lymington 23344
Hayter Bros., 1-spanner, *tel.* Lymington 23122
Campsites: Hollands Wood, 2-pennants, *tel.* Cadnam 3494.

Buckland Rings, Hampshire

See key map

To the west of the A337, 1 mile north of Lymington, is Buckland Rings, an ancient earthwork fortification. It predates Roman occupation although it is almost certain that there was a large garrison here as coins dating to Hadrian's time are occasionally unearthed in the area. Strategically the camp is in a good position to guard Silver Street, one of the feeder tracks to the Lymington Ridgeway and an old fording point on the Lymington River now about 500yds from the earthworks. The Rings are almost completely overgrown by trees, bramble and bracken and there is even a house built inside the fortification, but careful scrutiny will reveal the ditch and wall to the keen eye.

New Park Agricultural Shows

Some 240 acres in a field system, 1 mile to the north-west of Brockenhurst and bordered by the A337, New Park is the site of many equestrian events and specially-staged shows. The area was created in 1670 by Charles II as a royal deer park to replace the ancient enclosure south-east of Lyndhurst which had existed since the late 13th century. Horse trials, gymkhanas and tattoos are held each year by arrangement with the Forestry Commission; the largest of which, the New Forest Show, takes place on the last Wednesday and Thursday of July annually. It is a prestigious event for the Forest, and combines the attractions of horticultural, agricultural and livestock shows with lighter events such as domestic pets, small-holding and Forest produce, competitions and trading. The Forestry Commission take a large enclosure to show the work being achieved in this and other forests in the country, and there is usually a contest between forest workers to chop down a tree in the shortest time possible and convert it into fencing staves.

The wide main street at Buckler's Hard

Buckler's Hard, Hampshire

Map Ref: 14SU4000

Now just a few houses which line each side of an unusually wide central street, Buckler's Hard was once a thriving shipyard that contributed three men-o'-war to Nelson's fleet at Trafalgar among a total of 71 ships built here from 1745 to 1822. The main street, closed to traffic, is designed to be wide enough for whole New Forest oak logs to be rolled directly down to the 'hard' or slipway, on which the wooden ships were crafted. Around the settlement, which contains the fine house of master ship-builder Henry Adams (now a hotel), the trees were stacked roof-high to season. Ships were built here before Napoleonic times – the first yard was established at this idyllic spot on the Beaulieu River some 50 years earlier by John, Duke of Montagu, to build slave ships which would bring home sugar from the West Indies, a venture which failed when French settlers took over the islands. Today Buckler's Hard is one of the many tourist attractions of the Beaulieu Estate. Families heading for the Buckler's Hard car park should beware – the parking fee is charged per person in the car (£1 for adults, 50p for children) and not per vehicle. It is cheaper to walk from Beaulieu! The maritime museum displays many aspects of the shipwright's art including a detailed model of the 64-gun *Agamemnon* built here, a mainstay of the fleet at Trafalgar. The waterfront is alive with leisure yachtsmen preparing their craft for days in the Solent or longer trips to France and boat-trips along the Beaulieu River set off from one of the quays. Buckler's Hard was not the only shipyard on the river – nearby are Gilbury Hard, Bailey Hard and Carpenter's Dock.

AA recommends:
Hotels: Master Builder's House, Buckler's Hard, 2-star, *tel.* Buckler's Hard 253

Burley, Hampshire

Map Ref: 8SU2103

A pretty Forest village having strong associations with hunting and horseriding. There are several stables in the immediate area. The village pub, the Queen's Head, sports numerous hunting trophies and it is here that enthusiasts and horsemen gather before moving off. Stretching to the west are miles of open heathland – good walking country – and one of the Forest's few vantage points at Castle Hill. It was a defence encampment in pre-Roman times, but these days it is used by those wishing for a panoramic view over the Forest, the Avon valley, and the hills of Wiltshire and Dorset beyond.

AA recommends:
Hotels: Burley Manor, 3-star, Country House Hotel, *tel.* Burley 3314
Moorhill House, 2-star, Country House Hotel, *tel.* Burley 3285
Restaurants: White Buck, Bisterne Close, 2-forks, *tel.* Burley 2264

Cadnam, Hampshire

Map Ref: 3SU2913

Villagers enjoy quieter days and nights since the M27 was laid, and although it goes no farther than the south-west of Cadnam at present, the motorway does relieve the formerly hard-pressed A31 from Romsey and A336 from Southampton of much of their traffic. Motorists bound for the upper Avon and Wiltshire, for Lyndhurst, or for the busy A31 to Ringwood, which the motorway will eventually replace, are led well away from the centre of Cadnam, at the expense of some virgin forest, but the scars of roadworkings have healed fast. Conveniently nearby is Cadnam's famous pub, the Sir John Barleycorn, a large thatched inn, which enjoys particularly busy trading in summer months.

AA recommends:
Restaurants: Le Chantecherc, *tel.* Cadnam 3271
Garages: Kibbles, 2-spanners, *tel.* Cadnam 2204
Cadnam, 1-spanner, *tel.* Cadnam 2250

Castle Hill, (Godshill) Hampshire

Map Ref: 1SU1616

A plateau of high ground which runs south of Woodgreen and north of Godshill, Castle Hill forms the New Forest boundary for its one-mile length. Near Godshill are ancient

earthworks believed to be one of the few relics of Norman fortification, although, of course, William the Conqueror's peaceful contributions, and indeed the Forest itself, are everywhere in this part of Hampshire. A car park and two viewpoints along the ridge overlook the lazy bends of the River Avon on one side and the glades of Godshill Inclosure to the east.

Christchurch, Dorset

See key map

Idyllically placed between the estuaries of the rivers Avon and Stour, Christchurch is first mentioned in the Domesday Book as Twynham. The subsequent building of the Priory Church, started in about 1100 and finished in 1492, brought about the change in name. The Priory Church is a fascinating blend of styles and ages of architecture; the 118ft long nave and mighty arcades are Norman, as is the ornate turret in the north transept, while other parts, such as wood carvings in the choir stalls, are 15th century. There was also a castle here once, but all that remains are the walls of the keep. The Constable's House, of a similar vintage, has fared better. The hall, complete with its original windows, is intact and open daily to visitors.

Yachtsmen are attracted to Christchurch Harbour and so too are sea anglers, for not all fishermen are tempted by the game prospects of the Stour and Avon. The old quay which used to witness the arrival of sailing barges stacked with coal and timber now dispatches charter boats bound for

The Queen's Head at Burley; everybody's favourite watering place

the main fishing spots of the Solent. Mudeford, just across the Harbour, is a favourite place for sea-wall fishing and like Friar's Cliff and Highcliffe, further east, is also a popular seaside resort. There are numerous riverside walks in Christchurch and a nature trail across a wildfowl and nature reserve at Stanpit Marsh. The Red House Museum in Quay Road, formerly the workhouse, keeps a record of the town's social and natural history and has an aquarium, art gallery and gardens. There are other diversions: Tucktonia in Stour Road is a four-acre model of Great Britain with

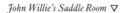

Christchurch Priory, seen across the river △   John Willie's Saddle Room ▽

Saddlery in the New Forest

To many people New Forest means only ponies and horses, and indeed the area is Britain's number one provider of mounts bred in the wild and in studs. To keep all that horse-power under control the arts of saddlery and harness-making have been re-established at Burley on the Forest's western edge. John Willie's Saddle Room, Ringwood Road, Burley is not only a shop for all the trappings of equestrianism – it is a thriving centre where saddles and harness are made by skilled craftsmen using traditional methods and materials.

Established in 1959 by Priscilla Serjeant and named after her Shetland pony, John Willie, the saddlery now employs five full-time saddlers and harness-makers fashioning the leather, tooling it for decoration and painstakingly hand-stitching the many styles of equipment. The saddlery began with one fully-experienced saddler and the other four workers have been trained in this once-dying craft. Only one college in Britain gives the theory training required – the Cordwainers Technical College, appropriately enough in Mare Street, Hackney, London. Mrs Serjeant's fledgling saddlers spend a year there before completing two further years back in the New Forest to gain their professional status, a training scheme sponsored by the Council for Small Industries in Rural Areas.

Her family's interest in competitive driving – the art of coaxing pairs or fours of horses and a carriage through a tough manoeuvring course (favourite sport of the Duke of Edinburgh) – led to the manufacture of two- and four-wheeled exercise carts and competition carriages, as well as a specialisation in functional but ornamented show harness. Carriage chassis are partly made in Bournemouth, and the most skilled work of all, that of the wheelwright, is carried out by a craftsman in Romsey – two further local inputs to a product finished at Burley.

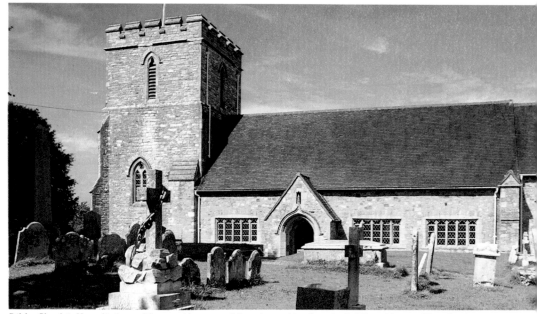

Dibden Church in Hampshire's peaceful countryside was one of the early casualties of war △ *Red House Museum, Christchurch* ▽

buildings and countryside scaled down in size but fully animated, and there are sailing, golf, squash, and riding clubs in the area.

Denny Lodge, Hampshire

Map Ref: 7SU3606

Britain's largest parish by area, Denny Lodge extends down almost all the New Forest's eastern edge from just south of Ashurst, to a point only two miles from the coast at the Beaulieu River mouth. Much of Denny Lodge, which is named after the former Groom Keeper's house some three miles south-east of Lyndhurst, is open heath and grassland interspersed with bogs and small copses. Its eastern edge is marked by a number of new plantations designed to screen off the industrial shore of Southampton Water. To the west are the older woodlands of the Denny and Denny Lodge Inclosures in a tract of forest stretching to Hollands Wood on the A337 Lyndhurst to Brockenhurst road. Denny has lent its name to one of the

main strains of New Forest pony which includes elements of Welsh stock brought into the Forest in the early part of this century. Named after a renowned stallion 'Denny Danny', the strain is characterised by a black coat and yellow eyes.

Denny Wood Campsite, Hampshire

Map Ref: 7SU3306

A minimum facility Forestry Commission campsite to which campers must bring their own toilets, located to the south of the B3056 1½ miles west of Beaulieu Road Station, 2¼ miles east of Lyndhurst. The site, from which dogs are barred, is on the edge of one of the Forest's largest wooded areas including Denny Inclosure and Lodge, Parkhill and Hollands Wood, through which a number of well-defined tracks run. It is a good centre for visits to the pony sales (Beaulieu Road Station), Lyndhurst and Beaulieu. Tickets can be obtained from the warden on arrival or first thing the next morning.

Dibden, Hampshire

Map Ref: 12SU4008

A tiny hamlet nestling in rolling country between Southampton Water and the Forest's eastern edge, Dibden is dwarfed by its neighbour, modern Hythe. In air attacks on waterside installations during the war it was Dibden church that became one of the early casualties. All Saints has been rebuilt on the 13th-century foundations with its original font intact – today's bells were recast from the metal of the bomb-damaged old bells.

Avon Beach, Christchurch ▷

The Portuguese Fireplace, near Emery Down, marks a spot once occupied by Portuguese troops

Eling, Hampshire

Map Ref: 7SU3612

A quiet backwater dwarfed by Totton, Britain's largest village, and by Red Bridge, which carries the busy A336 and A35 over the mouth of the River Test from Southampton to the New Forest and Bournemouth. Bartley Water drains into the Test estuary at Eling and is part-tidal, supporting one of only three tide mills in working order. On the hill above the mill stands St Mary's Church which contains an arch built before the Norman invasion of 1066. Below the church is Goatee Picnic Park and nearby a slipway and shingle foreshore, from which small craft on the estuary and the industry of Southampton's Millbrook trading estate are visible.

Emery Down, Hampshire

Map Ref: 6SU2808

Not far from Lyndhurst, the hamlet of Emery Down is within reach of some of the best known Forestry Commission walks of the New Forest, namely Radnor, with its sight of the Radnor Stone carved with scenes of the Forest wildlife and flora; the arboretum, which , as its name implies, follows plantations of varied and sometimes rare species of tree, and Mark Ash Walk, these three being called collectively the Bolderwood Forest Walks. But anglers probably know Emery Down better for the Leominstead Trout Fisheries; a tranquil, privately-owned lake stocked with brown and rainbow trout. Along the unfenced secondary road out of the village towards the A31 and Ringwood, near Millersford Bridge, is a recently restored Portuguese Fireplace; it marks the spot where buildings occupied by Portuguese troops once stood during World War I. Nearby is

Eling Tide Mill, Hampshire

Eling Tide Mill is the only mill in the country worked by tidal water *and* proving a commercial success. Harnessing two tides a day, mill manager and miller Tom Freestone's 12-hour day is worked in four-hour bursts of activity. The mill's sea-hatches (sluice-gates) are opened before the tide sweeps up Southampton Water and into the Eling Channel of Bartley Water past the mill and tollbridge as far as Rum Bridge (A35 road-bridge). The sluices are closed once high tide is reached, about four hours later. As the tide ebbs, and the channel drains out of the sea, Tom is left with a head of water, and with the sluices reopened, the power to drive his twin millstones by an undershot waterwheel running in a millrace.

The main advantage of a tidal mill over a conventional water mill is that tides are not subject to weather conditions. Eling Mill has no fear of the water drying up in a drought summer – which means milling for up to eight hours a day every day throughout the year.

With the current trend towards natural foodstuffs, Eling Tide Mill's 100% stoneground flour, sold as Canute brand by small health food shops, is much in demand and production since the mill was restored and opened in 1980 has more than doubled. With a full-time assistant and a trainee miller, Tom Freestone has recently diversified into animal foodstuffs. He has repaired formerly redundant 1920s machinery which will crush oats for New Forest ponies and local smallholders' goats and this will keep the mill financially viable during the winter when it is closed to visitors.

The mill was bought from Winchester College by New Forest District Council and restored after a 40-yr period of dereliction. So bad was its condition that practically all the foundations from the river bed upwards had to be replaced. Visitors are shown a fascinating audio-visual display on the stages of work carried out. Open Wednesday to Sunday inclusive, April to October, with a small admission fee.

the Holidays Hill Reptiliary, a Forestry Commission-owned collection of breeding amphibians and reptiles native to the Forest. Slow worms, lizards, frogs and less harmless adders can be studied from a safe distance except in winter, when most species hibernate.

Exbury, Hampshire

Map Ref: 14SU4200

Near the east bank of the Beaulieu River is the tiny village of Exbury, dominated, in early summer, by the vibrant colours and fragrances of Exbury Gardens. Between early April and mid June, garden-lovers can walk among the magnificence of some 250 acres of rhododendrons, azaleas and camellias in full bloom in the grounds of Exbury House, which is owned by a branch of the de Rothschild family. At nearby Lepe, a stretch of Solent foreshore is protected from the onslaught of industrialisation which has affected much of Southampton Water and the coast. It has been designated an Area of Outstanding Natural Beauty and a country park administered by Hampshire County Council. It is open for the harmless pursuits of sunbathing and swimming. There are fine views of Solent water traffic from the low cliffs above a shingle beach which attracts picnicking families and sea anglers. Lepe beach could well have been the point from which early Forest dwellers set out for the Isle of Wight. Fascinating prehistoric 'finds' have been dug up in the area, including Stone Age implements and the bones of an elephant.

The Esso refinery at Fawley

Fordingbridge, Hampshire

See key map

As its name implies, this was an important crossing point on the River Avon in years gone by, as the river, although quite wide, was quite shallow here. For many years villagers and travellers used a ford, but in the 14th century a seven-arched bridge was built which can still be seen today, preserved as an ancient monument. A more recent memorial is a life-size bronze of the artist Augustus John who died here in 1961; it overlooks the Avon and the Forest beyond, which he so loved. A busy little town, particularly in summer, when day-trippers and campers from nearby Sandy Balls campsite swell the shopping population.

AA recommends:
Hotels: Ashburn Hotel, 2-star, *tel.* Fordingbridge 52060

Fritham, Hampshire

Map Ref: 2SU2314

Fritham House and Lodge, a private school, farm and collection of attractive houses and country cottages make up the village which is bounded on all sides by forest and heath. Between Fritham and the A31 Cadnam to Ringwood road are the tarmacadamed ribbons of a disused wartime airfield, long abandoned for their original purpose, but very much in use today as car parks and unofficial circuits for learner-drivers. One of the Forest's several fishing spots is at Janesmoor pond (by permit only), and the

observant can determine several tumuli in the area, of which The Butt, near New Farm, is the most remarkable, and probably belongs to the Bronze Age. The Forestry Commission have allocated space for campsites both at the old airfield and at nearby Long Beech.

Godshill, Hampshire

Map Ref: 1SU1714

Just on the western edge of the New Forest boundary and 1¾ miles east of Fordingbridge, this little village is set among miles of open heathland and marvellous walking country. There are two car parks for those trekking across Godshill Ridge or Ditchend Bottom and, on warmer days, the plantation at Pitts Wood Inclosure provides welcome shade after the open scrub and gorse. Sandy Balls Holiday Centre provides 120 acres of level, sheltered grass for touring caravans and tents and in addition has static vans for hire. Facilities include hot and cold showers, mains electricity hook-ups, outdoor swimming pool and pony trekking.

Hampton Ridge, Hampshire

Map Ref: 1SU1913

One of the ancient ridgeways of the Forest, Hampton Ridge bore tradesmen 'exporting' New Forest ware – pottery made from clays of the area's north-west edge between the Avon valley and Fritham. Although few of the actual pottery sites have been found in the main areas of manufacture – around the Ditchend and Latchmore Brooks – products which have been identified as belonging to these sites have been found in excavations up to 50 miles north of the Forest. A major haul was unearthed on the site of a Roman camp outside Old Sarum. The present Forest paths which follow the Hampton Ridge route run from Abbots Well (just outside Frogham village) over Coopers Hill to join the Lymington Ridgeway at Bramshaw Telegraph.

Holbury, Hampshire

Map Ref: 12SU4303

Sandwiched between the eastern perimeter of the New Forest and the grey containers and pipework of Fawley Oil Refinery, near Southampton Water, is the small residential village of Holbury. Most of its inhabitants work either at the refinery, or at the power station at Marchwood, further along the foreshore towards Totton. Because of its isolation and large population, Holbury has become self-contained for shops and amusements, and has the only cinema in the immediate New Forest area.

Fordingbridge's seven-arched namesake is now an ancient monument

Holidays Hill Campsite, Hampshire

Map Ref: 5SU2706

A small minimum facility campsite deep in a woodland valley about ¼ mile from the A35 at New Forest Gate House and ¾ mile south-east of the 157ft hillock called Holidays Hill. Campers are expected to provide their own toilets. Tickets are to be obtained from the warden on arrival or first thing the next morning. The site is close to the Forestry Commission's reptiliary, the Rhinefield Ornamental Drive and the deep woodlands of Holidays Hill, Wooson's Hill and the Knightwood Inclosure. No dogs are allowed on this site.

Hollands Wood, Hampshire

Map Ref: 10SU3004

Just over a square mile of woodland lying to the east of the A337 one mile north of Brockenhurst is named Hollands Wood. Grazed by ponies and cattle, this old, deciduous woodland is self-regenerating. But one unnatural factor may intrude in its future – Hollands Wood also contains the Forestry Commission's second largest top category New Forest campsite, open from April to September to take a maximum of 600 tents, caravans and motor-caravans, three toilet blocks, chemical toilet disposal points, a childrens' adventure playground and a Forest information centre. Bookings for this popular venue can only be made for the Spring Bank Holiday period. The main site track follows the course of an ancient route from

Lymington to Ashurst along which sea-salt was carried from the coast.

AA recommends:
Campsites: Hollands Wood Campsite, Brockenhurst, 2 pennants, *tel.* Cadnam 2888

Holmsley Campsite, Hampshire

Map Ref: 8SZ2199

The Forestry Commission's largest campsite in the New Forest area, Holmsley Camp is on the dispersal area of one of the Forest's largest wartime airfields just off the A35 south of Holmsley Inclosure. The site, which has 700 pitches, is fully equipped with toilets (including facilities for the disabled) and a shop for most camping and caravanning requirements. Booking is required for the Spring Bank Holiday only. The southernmost site in the Forest, Holmsley is close to the coast (Highcliffe 4 miles) and is in an area of many small copses called 'hats'. To the north of the site is a large expanse of natural heath combining Dur Hill Down, Bisterne Common, Holmsley Ridge and Whitten Bottom with several well-defined walks providing some quite remote scenery. The name Holmsley is derived from the ancient word for holly, a tree found in profusion in many of the nearby copses.

Oil and natural gas in the New Forest

The widening of the search for oil and natural gas on the mainland of Britain has seen intense activity by exploration companies throughout Hampshire and Dorset, with substantial finds in the Basingstoke area joining the known resources at Wych Farm, Dorset. However, geologists regard the area of the New Forest as one of the next most likely areas in which this valuable resource could be extracted. Geological and seismological surveys have already pointed to the possibility of oil pockets existing in rocks under the Denny Lodge area of the woods.

Oil and gas are products of the compression and underground heating of deposits of marine animals and primitive sea plants. So an essential factor in the discovery of onshore oil is that underlying rock formations have at some stage in prehistory formed the sea-bed. Geologists then also look at the bending configuration of the rock strata, the pressure and temperature stresses they have undergone and the actual age of the rock, all clues to the possibility that the degradation of organic remains has resulted in the entrapment of oil in small recoverable pockets. Such formations are believed to exist in the New Forest and the next stage of exploration would be to drill test bores to determine the existence of oil and then whether or not it would be viable to extract it.

However, the exploration company concerned, Shell, ran up against a powerful army of conservation-minded bodies and people in pursuing an application to make test bores in Denny Inclosure, a woodland 2 miles south-east of Lyndhurst. Private individuals and local organisations of the New Forest objected on the grounds of amenity, noise, increased vehicle traffic, the possibility of well blowouts, visual intrusion and many other factors. As a result the application was turned down and it may be many more generations before the existence of oil is confirmed.

Keyhaven is a sheltered backwater on the Solent coast

Hurst Castle, Hampshire

See key map

It is not difficult to imagine how powerful a position Hurst Castle once commanded. Built at the end of a long spit of shingle extending well into the Solent, it was an obvious choice of site for coastal defence in the days of great sea battles. Henry VIII had Hurst Castle built around 1540; it was designed as a 12-sided tower surrounded by a garrison wall and meant to be as difficult to capture as it was to escape from, since the Cromwellians imprisoned Charles I here in 1648 before his (fateful) trial. Ever since, it has been put to use in some way or other in times of national need or emergency, most recently in the last World War as a sea and air observation post. Open to the public most weekdays and on Sunday afternoons, Hurst Castle can be reached either by ferry from Keyhaven, or on foot along the beach, a distance of about 1½ miles. This beach is a favoured spot for beach-casting and rewarding catches of cod, codling and bass are recorded each year.

Hythe, Hampshire

Map Ref: 12SU4208

Facing the mighty Southampton Docks across Southampton Water, with the New Forest on its back doorstep, Hythe is a pleasant dormitory town. A popular commuter route to Southampton is by sea; a regular ferry service leaves Hythe pier for Southampton's Royal Pier, which is close to the city's business and commercial centre. Hythe's pier is 100 years old and one of the longest in the country, so most regular ferry users catch a small train to the landing stage rather than walk its length. In the 1930s, Hythe was the embarkation point for Imperial Airways flying boat services to all parts of the world.

AA recommends:
Garages: Berkeley, Southampton Road, 2-spanners, *tel.* Hythe 843036

Keyhaven, Hampshire

See key map

A quiet and unspoilt backwater just outside the Forest boundary, Keyhaven attracts Solent yachtsmen, sea anglers and holidaymakers wishing to enjoy both sea and Forest. Yachtsmen call in from the hectic Solent for rest and repairs and there are two sailing schools using the safety of Keyhaven Lake and the sheltered jetties and slipway. This is also where keen anglers charter boats to take them to Shingles Bank, a bass ground which extends from Hurst Castle into the Solent. A small ferry takes sightseers to Hurst Castle, a Tudor garrison at the end of a spit of land. To one side of the tiny village of Keyhaven are marshes which are a sanctuary for species of seabirds and waterfowl, while to the west are the fine beaches and wider attractions of Milford-on-Sea.

AA recommends:
Self-catering: Fishers Mead Cottages and Flats, *tel.* Milford-on-Sea 2047

Linwood Farm Campsite, Hampshire

Map Ref: 4SU1809

A small private campsite on the Forest's western edge, situated on the minor road from the Avon Valley (off the A338 at Elingham Cross ¾ mile south of Ibsley) to the A31 at Slufters Inclosure. It is the Broomy Walk area of the Forest and is a good base for exploration of Milkham Inclosure, the sites of Roman pottery kilns in the Dockens Water valley and the woodlands of Appleslade and Red Shoot.

Long Beech Campsite, Hampshire

Map Ref: 3SU2512

A minimum facility (toilets provided) site, operated by the Forestry Commission situated at Long Beech, to the east of the minor road from the main A31 to Fritham. The site is reached by a Forest road suitable for caravans. Tickets can be obtained from the gate during the day but late arrivals should obtain them first thing the following morning. The site is ideally situated for the exploration of the Fritham area and the Bolderwood Walk.

Lymington, Hampshire

Map Ref: 13SZ3295

Isle of Wight ferry port, shopping centre and yachting haven, Lymington is a bustling, colourful town at the mouth of the Lymington River. Many of the graceful Georgian buildings lining the broad main street were built by families made rich by local salt gathered from the Salterns along the coast, and before this boat building was the main industry. In Victorian times, with the coming of the railway, it became a popular resort, and these days Lymington is best known for its ferry service which takes cars and passengers across the Solent to Yarmouth on the Isle of Wight. Small boats and yachts are still built, and the tidal Lymington estuary is choked with hundreds of small craft. Ships' chandlers pepper the quayside and a good selection of shops, plus a Saturday market, makes the town a good re-stocking centre for both

Lymington's streets have many interesting nooks and crannies

The Isle of Wight ferry in Lymington River

Lymington quay is a meeting place for yachtsmen – small boats are still made here

yachtsmen and holidaymakers. The harbour also sees a lot of fishing activity. It is from here that anglers hire boats to take them to the Solent's happy hunting grounds for bass, in particular. Tackle shops also sell the necessary day tickets for trout fishing the reaches of Lymington River.
St Thomas's Church at the top of the High Street has 18th-century galleries and an unusual roof – a tower crowned by a dome. The town has a large open-air swimming pool and a sports ground.

AA recommends:

Hotels: Passford House, Mount Pleasant, 3-star, Country House Hotel, *tel.* Lymington 682398
Angel, 108 High Street, 2-star, *tel.* Lymington 72050
Stanwell House, 2-star, *tel.* Lymington 77123
Restaurants: Fagin's, 135 High Street, 1-fork, *tel.* Lymington 73074
Limpets, 9 Gosport Street, 1-fork, 1-rosette, *tel.* Lymington 75595
Self-catering: 33, 36 & 37 Rodbourne Close, Everton, *tel.* Milford-on-Sea 2093

Lymington Ridgeway

In pre-Roman times the areas immediately north and south of Salisbury Plain were the most populous and industrious in Britain and the movement of people and goods between settlements considerable. The paths and tracks used by these early voyagers and salesmen were sited on the highest ground for several important reasons. Trees are much thinner on high ground, it is easier to get one's bearing on distant objectives, there are few streams or rivers to ford and travellers would be less vulnerable to surprise attack. Thus the main routes were ridgeways.

Not only does the New Forest stand astride direct routes from ancient port settlements on the coast but it had many products to contribute to prehistoric economy – pottery, salt and iron had to be transported to markets in the north and west. The Forest's main route was undoubtedly the Lymington Ridgeway, many parts of which now form modern roads through the area – other sections are still clearly marked by footpaths, bridleways and ancient earthworks.

At its southern end the first signs of the Ridgeway are found near the salterns (salt-drying pans) of Woodside, close to Lymington River mouth. It skirts Lymington itself on the route of minor roads to Sway and directly north-west to the Naked Man tree (qv) before being lost for a short space between Wilverley Post on the A35 and Burley Golf Course. Here it picks up the road to Picket Post where it swings north-east on the line of the A31 to the edge of Slufters Inclosure. Although there are minor roads that now follow a line to the next main mark, a tumulus known as The Butt, the old ridgeway probably crossed the area of the disused Fritham airfield before swinging north and joining the track of what is now the B3078 as far as Morgan's Vale. The Lymington Ridgeway leaves the New Forest here and continues north to join the major South Hants Ridgeway.

Several minor routes have been identified that join up with the Lymington Ridgeway to swell the volume of traffic. From the west is the Hampton Ridgeway (qv) and from the east the Saxon or Cloven Way connecting Nomansland with Golden Cross. Much of the Ridgeway can be followed by car and short lengths on foot – there are particularly fine views of the Avon valley and the Forest from Picket Post and the B3078 at Bramshaw Telegraph.

Lyndhurst, Hampshire

Map Ref: 6SU2908

'Capital' of the New Forest and its centre of administration since the 14th century, Lyndhurst lies among the mixture of open heathland and dense forest so typical of this part of Hampshire. To the north at Pikeshill is the source of the Beaulieu River, to the east, the breezy open spaces of Bolton's Bench (named after Lord Bolton, a Lord Warden of the Forest in 1688), White Moor and Matley Heath where there are ample car parks, official picnic spots and informal Forestry Commission campsites. To the west are miles of deep woodland, much of it planted many decades ago. This includes the Knightwood Oak. With a girth of 21 feet, it is one of the oldest (at about 600 years) and certainly the largest-girthed, oak trees in the Forest. South of Lyndhurst is New Park, the site of country, horticultural and agricultural shows, which was once a 200-acre royal deer park.

The most ancient part of the village itself is probably the 14th-century portion of the Verderers Hall which adjoins Queen's House Forestry Commission office. For centuries a Verderers Court has sat to administer justice within the Forest boundaries, and even today it is possible for a member of the public to make a 'presentment' or case on one Monday in every two months. Pubs, tea-rooms and souvenir shops attract more regular visitors, and in high summer Lyndhurst almost bursts at the seams. Major roads from Southampton and Cadnam converge here on their way to Lymington and Christchurch/Bournemouth, and although there is a one-way system, the main A35 eastbound funnels dense holiday traffic along its narrow main street. For those

Lyndhurst – home of the Forestry Commission and 'capital' of the New Forest

Lyndhurst Church has a beautiful east window designed by Burne-Jones

For succulent cuts of venison, John Strange's butcher's shop at Lyndhurst is the only source

Furzey Gardens boasts eight acres of trees and shrubs

Nomansland, Hampshire

Map Ref: 2SU2517

Curiously named because it was believed to be founded and built by squatters, this small village is bounded by the commons of Hamptworth, Landford and Plaitford. Nearby are car parks for walks and picnics in Bramshaw Wood, and there is a small, informal site for caravans run by the Forestry Commission at Piper's Wait.

Ocknell Campsite, Hampshire

Map Ref: 5SU2411

A small, water-tap only campsite on the dispersal area of a former World War II airfield, situated at the western edge of Ocknell Inclosure to the east of the

able to stop, a small Southern Tourist Board Information Centre in the main car park distributes information on the area and advice on accommodation bookings.

AA recommends:
Hotels: Crown, 3-star, *tel.* Lyndhurst 2722
Lyndhurst Park, 3-star, Country House Hotel, *tel.* Lyndhurst 2823
Parkhill, 3-star, *tel.* Lyndhurst 2944
Evergreens, 2-star, *tel.* Lyndhurst 2175
Pikes Hill Forest Lodge, 2-star, *tel.* Lyndhurst 3677
Forest Point, 1-star, *tel.* Lyndhurst 2420
Garages: New Forest Services, 3-spanners, *tel.* Lyndhurst 2861
Pats, 2-spanners, *tel.* Lyndhurst 2609
Restaurants: The Bow Windows, *tel.* Lyndhurst 2463

Matley Wood Campsite, Hampshire

Map Ref: 7SU3307

A Forestry Commission minimum-facility site in woodland on Matley Heath to the north of the B3056, 1¾ miles west of Beaulieu Road Station and 2 miles east of Lyndhurst. Campers are expected to provide their own toilets. Tickets can be obtained from the warden on arrival or first thing the following morning. Matley Wood is well situated for visits to the Beaulieu Road pony sales and exploration of the Lyndhurst and Denny area.

Minstead, Hampshire

Map Ref: 6SU2811

Most visitors to this maze of lanes and thatched cottages have either heard of the unusual church, or the curious inn sign outside the village pub. All Saints' Church looks more like a huddle of cottages than a place of worship; it dates from the 13th century, and has rarely-found features inside such as a three-decker pulpit and a series of wooden galleries called 'parlour pews'

which were reserved for the rich, influential families of the parish. The poor sat high under the roof in the Gipsies' Gallery. Sir Arthur Conan Doyle, creator of Sherlock Holmes, and his wife lie buried in the churchyard. Nearby at the crossroads stands the 'Trusty Servant' pub and the satirical sign which is based on a picture in Winchester College. It depicts the perfect servant: having the body of a pig to signify an unfussy eater, with a snout locked for secrecy, the ears of an ass, for patience, and a stag's feet for swiftness. In its left hand are a brush, shovel and a two-pronged fork – the tools of hard work. Furzey Gardens is a botanist's and gardener's delight, whatever the season. It consists of eight acres of flowering trees and shrubs in summer, evergreens and heathers in winter, and carpets of bulbs in springtime. Open daily, all year.

Naked Man, Wilverley

Map Ref: 9SU2401

A gaunt remnant of a once great tree, the Naked Man is a skeleton tree trunk guarded by railings on the north side of the Forest ride which marks the path of the Lymington Ridgeway as it runs beside Wilverley Inclosure. Many stories are told of this desolate old oak – although none come close to explaining its name. It is said that its thick boughs were a natural gallows where some of the Forest's highwaymen and smugglers caught trafficking in contraband from the coast to centres like Burley, were strung up by excisemen or the local forces of law and order led by the Riding Officer. However, the oak's great age, the loss of its bark and the bleaching of the wood by the prevailing weather suggest that at some stage in its history the dead trunk and boughs may have resembled a giant and ghostly naked figure. You will find the haunting remains a quarter of a mile south east of the A35 at Wilverley Post to the left of the Forest ride, a short walk from the Wilverley Plain car park.

Venison

The Strange family has owned and run the same butcher's shop in Lyndhurst's narrow main street for over 200 years. For much of that time, and particularly since the war, the shop has sold New Forest venison in a number of joints and cuts. John Strange, the present owner, thinks it has a rightful place among the more conventional meat he sells, and it is certainly a tourist attraction; but customers, who come from near and far, often need advice on how venison should be treated and cooked.

The game is available all year. Each April, it is a Forest Keeper's responsibility to count the head of deer on his particular beat. The census is important: too many can mean possible damage to tender young tree plantations or a risk to neighbouring landowners' crops, so numbers have to be contained. This is done by shooting, and all species of deer in the New Forest are subject to this control. John Strange puts in a tender to the Forestry Commission for the carcasses each year, and if successful, the shop handles several thousand whole carcasses a year.

At the shop, each carcass is butchered into joints and cuts in much the same way as lamb. The cheapest cut is ragoût (which compares to best end of neck in lamb) and the most expensive is breast (fillet of lamb). Boneless shoulder and leg are popular and meat trimmed off during butchery is used to make burgers, pâtés and sausages.

As venison is game, it is considered to taste better after a period of hanging – much like a pheasant or hare. All John Stange's venison is kept chilled (not frozen) and should be hung before cooking for between 7–10 days (according to taste) in a dry, airy place wrapped in muslin. Different cuts demand different cooking techniques, and the tougher ragoût meat, for example, needs slow, lengthy stewing, while a joint of leg may be roasted. One way of ensuring a succulent texture is to marinade the venison joint in a mixture of olive oil, diced vegetables, red wine and red wine vinegar; the oil and vinegar break down the fibres and the vinegar also imparts sharpness to an otherwise over-rich meat.

minor road to Fritham from the A31 at Stoney Cross Plain. Campers are expected to provide their own toilets. Tickets are to be obtained from the warden on arrival or first thing the following morning. The site is well situated for exploration of the Bolderwood Walk area of the Forest.

Piper's Wait, Hampshire

Map Ref: 2SU2416

About ½ mile north-east of the B3078, at a point halfway between Brook and Bramshaw Telegraph, is Piper's Wait, at 422ft the highest point within the New Forest Boundaries. A small hilltop within a clearing of heathland, Piper's Wait is reached by a short walk off the road to Nomansland. From here there are views to the Dean Hill crest of the South Hants Ridgeway in the north, Bramshaw Telegraph to the west and Bramshaw village to the east. From Piper's Wait you can take footpaths into the ancient and ornamental greenery of Bramshaw Woods.

In Two Beeches Bottom is the Piper's Wait Forestry Commission campsite, an informal caravan site with minimum facilities where campers are expected to provide their own toilets. It is reached by a track suitable for caravans from the minor road to Nomansland off the B3078 Cadnam to Fordingbridge road. Tickets are to be obtained from the warden on arrival or first thing the following morning. The northernmost of the Forest's campsites, Piper's Wait is an ideal base for exploration of the Bramshaw–Fritham area.

Rhinefield House, Hampshire

Map Ref: 9SU2603

Built in the late 19th century, Rhinefield House (2½ miles west of Brockenhurst on the Rhinefield Ornamental Drive) is on a site with a royal history stretching back to the 11th century. The first known building here was William the Conqueror's hunting

Bramshaw Wood, seen from Piper's Wait

Fishing on the River Avon

lodge, probably built over the ruins of a Roman brickyard and pottery. It became a fortified mansion used by John of Gaunt and, even later, the site of a hunting lodge frequented by Charles II. The present building, although designed in the Tudor style, dates only to the turn of the century. Lady Bowes-Lyon, now the Queen Mother, stayed here as did Germany's ruler, Kaiser Wilhelm II. Today the house is open on most days, enabling the public to view both the grand architectural style and the art and furnishings. The Armada dining room gets its name from a detailed carving of the Spanish fleet over the fireplace, which has a Grinling Gibbons surround.

Ringwood, Hampshire

See key map

Lying beside the River Avon on the western edge of the New Forest and east of the Dorset Moors, Ringwood was once a quiet market town favoured by retirement couples for its proximity to river, sea and Forest. Today it copes with a busy through-put of holiday traffic; the dual carriageways of the A31 Southampton to Bournemouth road slice it in two and roads from the upper Avon, north Dorset and Christchurch converge here. But there are still thatched cottages, markets on Wednesdays and the views from Hightown Common to compensate. Trout fishing on the Avon is available, although expensive, and the town offers other sporting facilities such as riding, golf, sailing and swimming. Ringwood and area have unhappy associations with the Royalists and the Civil War. The Duke of Monmouth was captured nearby while on his way to the coast and safety after the rebellion of 1685. Held at the White Hart Inn, he wrote to his uncle, James II pleading for clemency, but was refused. Two miles north of Ringwood is Ellingham where the unfortunate Dame Alicia Lisle lies buried in St Mary's churchyard. Having lost close members of her family in the war, she lost her own head, aged 70, on the ruling of the infamous Judge Jeffreys, accused of harbouring rebels after the Battle of Sedgemoor. The Lisle family

The country town of Ringwood is host to a busy market

ancestral home was at Moyes Court, east of Ellingham, which is now a school.

AA recommends:
Restaurants: Peppercorns, 9 Meeting House Lane, *tel.* Ringwood 78364/4361
Garages: J W Wells, Salisbury Road, 2-spanners, *tel.* Ringwood 6111
Robin Payne (Motor Engineers), Unit 5, Millstream Trading Estate, Christchurch Road, 2-spanners, *tel.* Ringwood 5588 & 77557

Roundhill Campsite, Hampshire

Map Ref: 11SU3302

Situated on Lodge Heath just south of the B3055, 2¼ miles east of Brockenhurst, Roundhill Campsite is Forestry Commission operated and has minimum facilities (toilets are provided). Tickets can be obtained from the warden on arrival or first thing the following morning. Roundhill visitors can choose between the dense woodlands to the north of the site with many through walks or the open aspects of Beaulieu Heath to the south for exploring forays. There is fishing (coarse) at the pond on Lodge Heath and many picnic areas around Beaulieu Heath, the nearest being at Stockley Cottage.

St Leonards Grange, Hampshire

Map Ref: 14SZ4098

A tiny hamlet on the west bank of the Beaulieu estuary within 1¼ miles of the sea, St Leonards Grange has a few houses clustered around the remnants of a former grange and chapel of Beaulieu Abbey some three miles to the north. The grange – or granary farm – would have been worked by the monks to supply the main community, and to save time and ensure they carried out their devotions, the farming brothers had their own place of worship.

Setthorns Campsite, Hampshire

Map Ref: 9SU2600

Setthorns (derived from Set Thorns, the name of a large nearby inclosure) is a small minimum-facility Forestry Commission campsite specially designed for use by lightweight, back-packing campers. It is situated by the side of the track of the ancient Lymington Ridgeway and close to an old (dismantled) railway off the minor road which follows the south edge of Wilverley Inclosure to Sway. On the Forest's southern edge, it is well-situated for forays to the coast at Christchurch as well as being near the Forest walks of Wilverley and Wootton. Campers can obtain tickets from the warden on arrival or first thing the following morning. Setthorns is the only New Forest site which is open all the year round.

Rhinefield Ornamental Drive

Lying north-west of Brockenhurst and off the A35, about 2½ miles out of Lyndhurst, is Rhinefield Ornamental Drive, one of the most popular features of the New Forest. Visitors can drive along an avenue of mature specimen trees, most of them planted in 1859. Fifty-seven of them had their heights and girths measured in 1974, when it was established that the Redwood, Black Spruce, Lawson Cypress, Red Spruce and Spanish Fir were the tallest of their species in Great Britain. It is possible to park (at either end of the Drive) and explore the species further on foot. There are three Forest walks, the short ½ mile Brock Hill Walk in the north; Blackwater Walk to the south, and the aptly-named Tall Trees Walk which follows the course of the Ornamental Drive on either side of the road for 1½ miles. The surface underfoot is specially graded for easy progress by pushchairs and wheelchairs, and narrator plaques along the route draw the walker's attention to items of particular interest. Not all the trees are mature: a freak hurricane in February 1974 badly damaged several species and these are gradually being replaced.

Brock Hill Walk is so-named after an oak- and beech-capped knoll which for centuries

Southampton, Hampshire

See key map

Gateway to the south of England and thriving container port, Southampton was virtually flattened by enemy bombs during World War II, yet it retains much of its ancient history. Intact are most of its medieval town walls and four gateways. Bargate, the northern gate, houses a museum of local history, and separates the popular shopping area of Above Bar from the High Street within the old city. The remains of the 12th-century South or Water Gate are at the other end of the High Street, and here, too, are the remains of the ancient Holy Rood church, which are preserved as a memorial to the Merchant Navy. Within the old town are most of the city's historic artefacts: close to the city's oldest church, St Michael's, which dates from the 11th century, is the Tudor House museum, an attractive building containing a banqueting hall with minstrel's gallery, an oak-panelled ceiling and the remains of an upper hall fireplace with round chimney and formal gardens in the Tudor 'Knot' style. The Maritime Museum is housed in the 14th-century Wool House, a reminder of the days when the city was one of the chief wool-exporting ports. Pride of place among the models of ships ancient and modern is given to the Queen Mary. God's House Gate, formerly a debtor's prison, houses the rewards of the city's archaeological excavations which include a collection of post-Roman European pottery, Saxon ceramics, Roman artefacts and tools dating from the Stone Age.

Southampton's Civic Centre is modern, and in addition to law courts, government offices and the city's

has been a badger sett. 'Broc' is old English for badger, and the Forestry Commission keeps a vigilant eye on the numbers living here so that their survival is safeguarded. This is an area of ancient oaks grown for timber production, with narrator plaques along the way. Rhinefield Ornamental Drive's third walk is skirted, in part, by the Blackwater River, which joins other streams to create the Lymington River. Ramblers can linger on several bridges crossing this stream, and see the new arboretum, planted in 1960, which will supplement the mature trees of another Ornamental Drive. at Bolderwood.

The name 'Rhinefield' is said to originate from the Old English 'Ryge feld', meaning the open land where rye was grown in fields surrounding the old lodge. Rebuilt in 1877 and renamed Rhinefield House, the old lodge was the home of the Master Keeper in 1715 and the Duke of Cambridge in 1811. In 1938 the county council adopted the forest track which gave access to the lodge as a public highway from Brockenhurst to the Lyndhurst to Bournemouth road. The land on either side of the Rhinefield Ornamental Drive was first enclosed in 1700, starting with Vinney Ridge Inclosure, where oak and beech are planted.

central library, houses an art gallery and guildhall where shows and concerts are held. The art gallery specialises in well-known British painters from the 18th century and Continental Old Masters, while the John Hansard Gallery at Southampton University exhibits contemporary art, photography and crafts.

The Pilgrim Fathers left from Southampton for America, and a tall stone memorial beyond the city's West Gate commemorates their departure in the *Mayflower* and *Speedwell* in 1620.

The city boasts excellent shopping facilities which are concentrated along the length of High Street and Above Bar. Sporting opportunities are diverse, too, and include a large swimming pool in Western Esplanade; an ice rink in Banister Road; and the Civic Sports Centre at Bassett, to the north of the city centre (this includes an athletics stadium with all-weather track, two golf courses, seven football pitches, five cricket grounds, twelve tennis courts, two bowling greens, a ski slope, putting greens and canoe lake). Gymnastics, basketball, badminton, squash and weight training are available at St Mary's Sports Hall in St Mary's Road, and for sports viewers, there is Hampshire County Cricket at Northlands Road and frequent

matches, in season, at Southampton Football Club's ground, The Dell.

The city has a lively selection of pubs, restaurants and night clubs, numerous cinemas and two theatres, the Gaumont in Commerical Road, and the Nuffield, University Road.

AA recommends:

Hotels: Polygon, Cumberland Place, 4-star, *tel.* Southampton 26401
Dolphin, High Street, 3-star, *tel.* Southampton 26178
Post House, Herbert Walker Avenue, 3-star, *tel.* Southampton 28081
Southampton Moat House, 119 Highfield Lane, 3-star, *tel.* Southampton 559555
Southampton Park, Cumberland Place, 3-star, *tel.* Southampton 23467
Albany, Winn Road, The Avenue, 2-star, *tel.* Southampton 554553
Atlantic, 28–30 Hill Lane, 2-star, *tel.* Southampton 24612
Star, High Street, 2-star, *tel.* Southampton 26199
Restaurants: Olivers, Ordnance Road, 2-forks, *tel.* Southampton 24789
Golden Palace, Above Bar Street, 1-fork, 1-rosette, *tel.* Southampton 26636
Garages: Berkeley, 21/33 St Denys Road, 3-spanners, *tel.* Southampton 559533
Criterion, Bitterne, 3-spanners, *tel.* Southampton 26907
Newmans, Redbridge Causeway,

3-spanners, *tel.* Totton 865021
Alex Bennett, 126–146 Portswood Road, 3-spanners, *tel.* Southampton 554081
Carey & Lambert, 75 The Avenue, 3-spanners, *tel.* Southampton 554081
F Halfpenny & Son, 102 High Road, Swaythling, 3-spanners, *tel.* Southampton 554346
Hendy Lennox, South Front, Palmerston Road, 3-spanners, *tel.* Southampton 28331
Lex Mead, Marsh Lane, 3-spanners, *tel.* Southampton 30911
Perrin Motors, 1 Marsh Lane, 3-spanners, *tel.* Southampton 35581
Picador Motor Co, Portsmouth Road, Sholing, 3-spanners, *tel.* Southampton 449232
R F Seward, 234 Winchester Road, 3-spanners, *tel.* Southampton 785111
Testwood Motors, Janson Road, Shirley, 3-spanners, *tel.* Southampton 779455
Wadham Stringer, 73 The Avenue, 3-spanners, *tel.* Southampton 28811

Southampton Water

The joint estuary of the Hampshire trout rivers Itchen and Test, Southampton Water is an 8½-mile-long funnel from the major docks of Southampton to The Solent at Calshot. It is along this vast natural gateway to the sea that the great liners of the past nosed out from Ocean Dock, destination the Atlantic. That last great remnant of the cruising age, the QE2, is still a regular visitor. But Southampton Water's main traffic, visible from several points on the eastern edge of the New Forest, is now in container ships, tankers which berth off the major oil refinery at Fawley, and ferries. Traversed by the Hythe ferry (from Southampton's Town Quay) the Water is also busy with major routes to Cherbourg and Le Havre as well as smaller craft heading for Cowes on the Isle of Wight. Fleetest users of this major waterway are the hydrofoils running between Royal Pier and Cowes.

Early users of the Water were the Romans, who established a port here to service Winchester, probably on the Itchen at Bitterne. Twelfth-century crusaders saw its shores as their last glimpse of Britain as did many of the soldiers embarked for the battlefield of Agincourt. And it is appropriate for a port that once provided the main connection to America for freight and passengers that the Pilgrim Fathers' vessels *Mayflower* and *Speedwell* were fitted out and crewed in the old port of Southampton.

Today Southampton Water is also a great water playground for weekend yachtsmen out of Calshot and the River Hamble mouth. At night the water is lit eerily by the flare stacks of the Fawley refinery and other industrial plants on the west shore. But there are still many unspoilt parts of the Water's shoreline including Netley Abbey Castle and Hamblecliff. Fishing provides good sport as far up as the waters of the Docks which contain some really ferocious conger eels.

The Tudor House Museum, Southampton

Stoney Cross Plain, part of which was once an airfield, is now a popular grazing place

Sowley Pond, Hampshire

Map Ref: 13SZ3796

An attractive wood-fringed lake only half a mile from the sea, Sowley Pond lies just south of the hamlet of East End. The lake was formed by damming water draining from Beaulieu Heath. Sowley Pond was once the site of a major ironworks supplying hardware to the shipwrights of Buckler's Hard and the Beaulieu River. The massive iron forging hammer was driven by a waterwheel operated by a mill-race at the outflow of Sowley Pond to the sea at Colgrims. The ironworks is now completely demolished and the site lies within the grounds of Sowley House.

Stoney Cross, Hampshire

Map Ref: 5SU2611

A small clutch of buildings on either side of the busy A31 Southampton to Ringwood road includes The Compton Arms, a Georgian-style hotel with its own hunting and riding stables. The road follows the ridge of a plateau of high moorland called Stoney Cross Plain, part of which was converted to an airfield in World War II. On the opposite side of the road from the hotel are footpaths and walks to Stricknage Wood and the Rufus Stone.

AA recommends:
Hotels: The Compton Arms, 2-star, *tel.* Cadnam 2134

Sway, Hampshire

Map Ref: 9SZ2798

A small village on the fringe of the New Forest with a halt on the Southampton to Bournemouth railway, Sway is three miles north-east of Lymington. The village is chiefly known for the local landmark of Peterson's Tower on the Arnewood estate. This 218ft edifice, which took over five years to build, is an early example of concrete-work finished almost 100 years ago. Locally it is regarded as a folly but it may well have been erected to try out techniques of concrete construction. The countryside around Sway features in Captain F Marryatt's *Children of the New Forest*.

AA recommends:
Hotels: White Rose, Station Road, 3-star, *tel.* Lymington 682754
Garages: Meadens, Durnstown, *tel.* Lymington 682212

Upper Canterton, Hampshire

Map Ref: 3SU2612

The village nearest the spot where, legend has it, King William II was fatally wounded by an arrow while buck hunting on 2 August, 1100. Like many historical accounts, the true story of King Will's death will never be known. Called 'Rufus' because of a shock of flaming red hair, he was not a popular man, being physically ugly with a character to match, and it is quite possible that his death was no accident. The Rufus Stone, which marks the spot where the King fell, was first erected in 1745 by the Earl de la Ware, but it soon became covered in graffiti and in 1841 was covered with a protective iron coating. Gravel car parks in the clearings cater for sightseeing traffic.

Woodgreen, Hampshire

Map Ref: 1SU1717

On the westward fringes of the New Forest, among the watermeadows of the Avon, this village once attracted country folk from near and far at fruit picking time. The area produced a particular variety of sweet black cherry called 'Merries' and so good were they to eat that 'Merry Sundays' became a celebrated tradition of tasting and general enjoyment. The trees are no longer flourishing, but a magnificent avenue of oaks are; they were planted along the Drove nearly 200 years ago during the Napoleonic Wars to provide timber for the Navy's warships in years to come. There is still more horticultural interest at The House of Flowers nursery where five acres are under glass and propagation.

The Forest and the Artist

The verdant peace of the New Forest has attracted many painters, writers and poets. Woodgreen's village hall received the attention of artists R W Baker and E R Payne in the early 1930s; they painted the inside walls with murals of everyday country life and such bygone scenes as children carrying pails of milk or singing hymns in the little chapel nearby have been recorded for posterity.

Lyndhurst appealed to the pre-Raphaelite painters. Its 19th-century church of St Michael and All Angels is enriched by the handiwork of Millais, Burne Jones and Lord Leighton and there is a fresco in the chancel by Hamilton Aide. Augustus John lived for the latter part of his life at Fordingbridge, and a life-size statue has been mounted to his memory.

Authors, too, came to the Forest for rest and inspiration. The most famous result is probably *Children of the New Forest* by F Marryatt, but R D Blackmore, Mrs Gaskell and Conan Doyle (who was buried at Minstead) used the area for background in their writings. And Lewis Carroll's great friend Alice Hargreaves, née Liddell, who he used as his model for *Alice in Wonderland* lies buried in the churchyard at Lyndhurst.

Angling, Freshwater

Allen's Farm Sandlehealth, Fordingbridge, Hants *tel.* (072 53) 313. Offers 4 landscaped lakes of around 4 acres in total, holding rainbow trout at an average size of 1lb 8oz, although 3lb specimens have been caught. There is a wooded stretch of quiet river well-stocked with brown trout, ranging from 12oz to 2lb 8oz. Fly fishing only – season 27 Mar–17 Oct. Although not stocked with particularly large trout the fisheries provide enjoyable sport in pleasant settings.

River Avon Noted waters offering some of the best salmon and coarse fishing in the South of England. In the spring salmon run up to 25lb each and fish of 40lb plus have been recorded. Salmon-fishing permits are obligatory. Applications to: Major J M Mills, Bistern Park, Ringwood *tel.* (042 54) 4246. Coarse fishing on the Avon is legendary and the river has excellent stocks of pike, barbel, chub, dace, roach and grayling. 20lb pike are not exceptional and fish in excess of 30lb have been noted. Although not introduced until 1900, the barbel has flourished and 14lb specimens bring anglers from far afield. Large chub and dace can be expected along with good-sized roach. The best stretch is between Sopley and Winkton. Daily tickets: Christchurch Angling Club, D Chislett, 9 Woodfield Road, Bournemouth. The Greyhound Hotel, Fordingbridge.

Beaulieu River The source is Matley Bog, 1m N of Lyndhurst. Best places for fishing are Cadnam's Pool, Hatchet Pond and Whitton Pond. The river holds bream, eel, perch, pike, tench and roach along its 11m course towards Buckler's Hard. Fishing permits from: The Forestry Commission, The Queen's House, Lyndhurst *tel.* (042 128) 2801 or local shops.

Damerham Lakes 1m S of Damerham village off B3078, Fordingbridge to Cranborne road *tel.* (072 52) 446. The fishery holds rainbow trout only, with an average size of 2lb 8oz. However, fish in excess of 8lb have been caught. Only fly fishing is permissible and imitative patterns have proved more successful than lures or streamers. The lakes are long and narrow and consequently the water tends to be very clear, making casting to rising fish relatively easy. Season 2 Apr–31 Oct with twice-weekly stocking.

Ringwood Varied fishing available locally, including Linford Water. Daily tickets: The Tackle Shop, Ringwood or Ringwood Angling Club.

Angling, Sea

Lymington Excellent estuary fishing, with tope and sting-ray at Thorn's Beach towards Beaulieu. Boats available throughout the year offering chances of cod, whiting, conger, skate, mackerel, porbeagle and thresher sharks. Trips to the Needles are a speciality. Details from: The Lymington & District Sea Fishing Club, Sec K F Baveridge, 51 Gore Road, New Milton.

Milford-on-Sea Good beach and small boat fishing for bass and mackerel.

Golfing

Whilst the New Forest region is not particularly known for its golfing associations, there are, nevertheless, a number of interesting courses for both the inexperienced and the seasoned golfer.

Barton-on-Sea Marine Drive, Barton-on-Sea *tel.* (0425) 615308. An interesting course designed by H S Colt. Players must contend with the typical windswept conditions associated with a seaside links. The 576-yard 12th hole is particularly difficult. Visitors from recognised clubs welcome. 18 holes, 5650yds, par 68. **Local hotels** Red House Hotel, Coastguard Hotel, Barton-on-Sea; Chewton Glen, New Milton.

Bramshaw Brook, Lyndhurst *tel.* (042 127) 3252. Choice of two courses. The Manor course which is basically parkland, and the New Forest course which is wooded with streams as natural hazards. Visitors welcome, societies catered for by arrangement. Both courses 18 holes, Forest 5753yds, par 69, Manor 5634yds, par 70. Planned improvements will alter scratch. **Local hotels** Bell Inn, Brook.

Bramshott Hill Dibden, Hythe *tel.* (0703) 845596. A parkland course designed by J Hamilton with fine views across Southampton Water. The tricky 3rd hole is well guarded by a pond. Visitors welcome. 18 holes, 6233yds, par 71. **Local hotels** Montagu Arms, Beaulieu.

Brockenhurst Manor Sway Road, Brockenhurst *tel.* (059 02) 3332. An attractive course set on the edge of the New Forest in woodland. Interesting features include two dog-legs on the 4th and 17th holes. The course was designed by H S Colt. Visitors from recognised clubs welcome. 18 holes, 6216yds, par 70. **Local hotels** Balmer Lawn Hotel, Forest Park Hotel, Rose & Crown, The Brockenhurst.

Burley A31 from Ringwood, turn right at Picket Post *tel.* (042 53) 2431. An undulating course set in heather

Fishing on the River Avon, near Ringwood

Everything for the equestrian can be found at John Willie's Saddle Room at Burley

and moorland. A good tee-shot is required at the tough 7th if par is to be achieved. Visitors welcome. 9 holes, 6140yds, par 69. **Local hotels** Burley Manor Hotel, Moorhill House Hotel.

New Forest Southampton Road, Lyndhurst *tel.* (042 128) 2450 A heather-bound course on high ground overlooking the village of Lyndhurst, designed by P Swann. Holes 1, 2 and 9 are particularly tricky and the course has the unusual natural hazard of Forest ponies. 18 holes, 5833yds, par 71. **Local hotels** Crown, Evergreens, Forest Point Hotel, Lyndhurst Park Hotel.

Hunting

Three packs hunt the district. The New Forest Fox Hounds from kennels near Minstead and the New Forest Buck Hounds both hunt the Forest's central region, whilst the New Forest Beagles operate in the northern part.

Riding & Trekking

The New Forest has long been famous for its ponies. Originally working horses for the foresters, these days the domesticated ponies are used almost exclusively for riding – being small and compact, they are ideal for children. The Forest has many riding schools, stables and studs, consequently the visitor to the area should have no difficulty in finding suitable facilities for all equestrian activities.

Barton Stables Drift House,

Holmsley Road, New Milton (Ms A M Child), 8 Powercourt Road, Barton-on-Sea *tel.* (0425) 612098.

Beacon Corner Burley (Ms D M MacNair) *tel.* (042 53) 2272.

Blunts Barch Children's Riding School (S Gorley) *tel.* (0425) 52435.

Burley Villa Riding School Bashley Common Road, Bashley *tel.* (0425) 610278.

Bramble Hill Hotel Bramshaw Riding Stables *tel.* (042 127) 2420.

Coakes Riding, Livery & Saddlery Centre Shirley Holms Farm House *tel.* (0590) 682667 or 682567. Facilities include riding holidays, hacking, hunting, tuition, side-saddle, a cross-country course, indoor school, day-rides featuring picnic, carriage hire, English or Western riding straight into the Forest.

Crown Wood Stables Emery Down, Lyndhurst *tel.* (042 128) 2730.

Decoy Pond Farm Near Ashurst, Lyndhurst *tel.* (042 129) 2652. Ideal for New Forest rides. No roadwork. Qualified instruction. Holidays available.

Forest Park Riding Stables Rhinefield Road, Brockenhurst *tel.* (0590) 23429.

Knight Bridge Riding, Training & Holiday Centre Sway, Lymington (Ms Harris) *tel.* (0590) 68227. Open all year round weekends or weekly. Groups (maximum 15). Full board with some dormitories available. Pony-trekking a speciality.

Matcham Park Stables 196 Hurn Road, Matchams *tel.* (042 54) 3484. Novice to advanced riding. Qualified instructors. Discounts for large organisations.

New Park Stables Midway between Lyndhurst and Brockenhurst on A337 *tel.* (0590) 23467. Trekking and riding holidays. Bar and restaurant. Approved by the ABRS.

West Beams Trekking Centre Sway Road, Brockenhurst *tel.* (0590) 23032. Residential riding holidays. Daily trekking. Hunting. Liveries taken.

Potteries and Crafts

Furzey Gardens, Minstead, are notable for the Will Selwood Art and Craft Gallery, where an average of 100 craftsmen and 50 artists who live and work in the New Forest are represented. Named after the father of the present owner of Furzey Gardens (which is a charitable trust), the Gallery offers all-comers the sought-after opportunity of getting their work seen and appreciated by the general public – and hopefully, sold. All work on display is accepted by the Gallery on a sale or return basis, and it is up to each craftsman or artist to display his work in a given area and to ring the changes with different stock and new creations every so often. All the Gallery asks is that both the idea and the work itself are original.

The range of work is wide, from wood sculpture through basket weaving, silver enamelled jewellery and pewter to porcelain. Part of the collection, chiefly larger items of wood turning and wrought iron, is housed in an ancient cottage built around 1560, itself the subject of skilful and artistic renovation. Occasionally the Gallery mounts an exhibition of one particular artist's work; the late Ron Lane's artistry in wood is always appreciated as he sculpted exquisitely detailed and lifelike carvings of animals such as a field mouse climbing a stalk of corn.

Like Furzey Gardens, the Will Selwood Art and Craft Gallery is open throughout the year from 10am to 7pm (or until dusk in winter) and closed for lunch between 1 and 2pm. An admission fee is charged.

Other New Forest potteries and craft workshops are: The Kristen Pottery and Craft Shop, High Street, Beaulieu. Specialises in hand-thrown domestic earthenware and figurines (open every day, including Sundays). Angel's Farm Pottery, Chapel Lane, Lyndhurst, also open all day every day. Sells a range of stoneware hand-thrown pots for practical and ornamental use. Secrets of the Forest, High Street, Beaulieu. Hand-made children's smocks, hand-woven tweeds, engraved glass and jewellery (open 10am–5pm Monday to Saturday). Fordingbridge Craft Gallery, Salisbury Street, Fordingbridge. Specialises in needlework accessories, corn dollies, leather goods, patchwork. Open Monday to Saturday, shop hours. Matchmaker, 1 High Street, Lymington; fabrics, pottery lamps and marine paintings by Hampshire artist Rodney Charman. Open Monday – Saturday, closed Wednesdays in winter.

Riding for the Disabled

Details may be obtained from the following:

Lyndhurst District Group (Ms W Kemish), 13 Queen's Road, Lyndhurst *tel.* (042 128) 3623.

New Forest Group (Mr J Spring), Windmill, Sandy Down, Lymington *tel.* (059 02) 3371.

Sailing

The key places for sailing in the New Forest area are the Lymington and Keyhaven rivers. Both have excellent facilities for building, mooring and repairing yachts.

Keyhaven River   Good sheltered waters which are in use throughout the season by the Keyhaven Yacht Club and the Hurst Castle Sailing Club. Both clubs boast very good facilities and the latter caters particularly for 18ft boats and under. Various regattas and handicap races are held on a regular basis.

Lymington River   All local waters are controlled by the Harbour Commissioners. However, events are held by the Royal Lymington Yacht Club and the Lymington Town Sailing Club. Regatta time is during August and September and includes a popular junior event. Handicap racing takes place throughout the year. There are two marinas on the river's western bank and local traders are on hand to supply stores, repairs and lying-up facilities. All four clubs serving the Lymington and Keyhaven Rivers regularly attend Cowes Week on the Isle of Wight.

Local launching points

Keyhaven   Concrete slipway with hard gravel access. Launching possible at most tides. Parking available.

Lymington (Bath Road)   Concrete slipway. Launching at all tides. Craft up to 25ft only. Parking with the permission of the Harbour Commissioners.

Lymington (Town Quay)   Slipway with launching only possible at high tides. Limited parking available.

Inland Sailing

Blashford Lake   Near Rockford, 1½m N of Ringwood. Home of the Spinnaker Club.

Places of interest

Ashurst
New Forest Butterfly Farm   Long Down, Ashurst, 3½m from Totton off A35 towards Bournemouth then 1m down signposted lane *tel.* (042 129) 2166. Butterfly reserve set in tropical gardens rich in banana and lemon trees, passion flowers and a host of

other plants and shrubs required by breeding butterflies. The many species represented come from as far afield as Africa, Australia, Asia and the Americas. A separate area houses British butterflies only. Scorpions, tarantula spiders, praying mantises, stick insects and leaf-cutting ants are among the weird and wonderful specimens that are safely kept behind glass. Other facilities include a tea-shop, putting green and picnic area. Open Apr–Oct 10–5 daily.

The Motor Museum at Beaulieu

Beaulieu Abbey, National Motor Museum and Palace House
The early 13th-century abbey and gardens are open throughout the year and an exhibition of early monastic life is situated at the entrance to the ruins. One of the finest museums of its type in the world containing examples of over 200 historic cars, commercial vehicles and motorcycles. The story of motoring is charted from its origins in the 1890s to the present day. *tel.* (0590) 612345. The Palace House has been the Montagus' family home since 1538 and houses an exhibition of ancestral costumes. General features include a monorail, miniature veteran car-rides, railway world in miniature, transporama, radio-controlled model veteran cars and rides on a pre-war London bus. Spacious refreshment area. Open all year – Easter–Sep 10–6. Oct–Easter 10–5.

Boldre. Spinners   2m N of Lymington. Botanical gardens featuring azaleas, rhododendrons, camellias, magnolias, etc. Woodland ground cover includes primulas and blue poppies. Rare plants and shrubs for sale. Open Apr–Aug (ex Mon) 2–7, no dogs *tel.* (0590) 73347.

Breamore Church   Rare Anglo-Saxon church built in the early 11th century and delightfully set among cedars. **Breamore House, Countryside and Carriage Museums**   Fine Elizabethan manor (1583) housing a superb collection of works of art including paintings, porcelain and tapestries. The Countryside Museum contains agricultural machines and examples of rural arts. The Carriage Museum houses the 'Red Rover' stage-coach among its many exhibits. Home-made

teas available. Open Apr–Sep (Tue, Thu, Sat & Sun) 2–5.30 *tel.* (0725) 22270 or 22468.

Brockenhurst Church   Norman/early English structure. Burial place of 'Brusher' Mills, a famous New Forest snake-catcher. The churchyard features a 1000-year-old yew tree. Rhinefield House: part Victorian/part Tudor mansion situated in very large grounds. Open all year daily 10–5.

Brook. Rufus Stone   1m W of Cadnam on B3078. Spot where William Rufus reputedly met his death in the 11th century.

Buckler's Hard. Cottage Displays   Depicting 18th-century life in the village at various levels, including a shipwright's cottage, a labourer's home and Henry Adams' workplace. Also featured is the New Inn as it was in 1793. **Maritime Museum**   nautical collection monitoring the ship-building history of the village. Special displays include Henry Adams Master Shipbuilder, Nelson's Favourite Ship, Buckler's Hard and Trafalgar, Shipbuilding at Buckler's Hard and the Sir Francis Chichester Exhibition.

Christchurch. Priory   Imposing church with Norman turret. Set in beautiful gardens. **Red House Museum Gardens**   Featuring roses, sub-tropical shrubs and an English herb-garden. Open Tue–Sat 10–5, Sun 2–5 *tel.* (0202) 482860.
Tucktonia: Stour Road, off the A35. Fascinating scaled-down models of famous British buildings, plus leisure complex consisting of amusement park, go-kart racing, bumper boats, giant slide and crazy golf. Open Mar–Oct from 10 *tel.* (0202) 482710.

Fordingbridge. Hale Park   A finely furnished Georgian mansion set in lovely gardens. Built by Thomas Archer in 1715 and remodelled by Henry Holland in 1770.

Lepe and Calshot Country Park   2m S of Fawley off A326. 120 acres of cliffs and foreshore above the Solent. Area of outstanding natural beauty, with excellent views of the Isle of Wight. Abundant with waterfowl.

Lymington. Buckland Rings   1m N of Lymington. An ancient Iron Age earthwork with triple rampart. Many Roman coins discovered nearby. **Culverlea House**   Pennington Common. An acre of gardens with various trees, shrubs and flowers *tel.* (0590) 73163. **Hurst Castle**   At end of a 1½m peninsula 4m S of Lymington. Coastal fortress built by Henry VIII.

Lyndhurst. Cuffnell's Park   Recreation area noted for its rhododendrons. **Knightwood Oak**   2m SW off A35. One of the oldest pollarded trees in the New Forest. **Reptiliary. Holidays Hill**   A35. Comprehensive collection

Butterflies galore flutter amid tropical gardens at Ashurst

of British reptiles and amphibians including adders, smooth snakes, frogs and toads. Open Apr–Sep. **Verderers Hall** Ancient seat of New Forest justice built in 1388, acting as a court for local offenders.

Minstead. Furzey Gardens 8 acres of botanical gardens which cost £7000 to develop in the 1920s. Main features include eucryphias, azaleas, embothriums and rhododendrons. **Furzey House** Attractively designed mansion built in 1922 by Boulton and Paul, boasting the largest thatched roof in the New Forest. **The Ancient Cottage** Small dwelling believed to be built in 1560. Visitors can glimpse the early life-style of a lowly forester. Timbers for the house are reputedly from the Tudor boat-yards at Lymington. **Will Selwood Gallery** Modern building of timber and thatch, aiming to perpetuate local skills and trades. The work of over 100 artists and craftsmen permanently on display. Open all year daily 10–7.

Ringwood. Ellingham Church 2m N of Ringwood. An interesting 18th-century church with a reredos believed to be by Grinling Gibbons. **Minquiers** 1½m SW off A31. 1½ acres of pleasant woodland gardens featuring magnolias, camellias and various heathers. Limited opening during May *tel.* (042 54) 2604.

Rockbourne. Roman Villa 2m NW of Fordingbridge. 73 rooms discovered to date, with excavation still taking place. Nearby museum contains displays of locally found pottery, jewellery and coins. Open Apr–Oct (Mon–Fri) 2–6, Sat, Sun & Bank Holidays 10.30–6 *tel.* (072 53) 445.

Romsey. Broadlands The Georgian home of the Mountbatten family, currently occupied by the young Lord and Lady Romsey. The Prince and Princess of Wales spent the first days of their married life here in 1981. The main building's many treasures include porcelain and sculptures. The William and Mary Stable houses an exhibition which depicts the life and times of the Mountbattens. Grounds are idyllically situated by the River

Test. Facilities include parking, picnic area, gift shop and restaurant. Open Apr–Sep 10–6 *tel.* (0794) 516878. **Romsey Abbey** 10th-century church with Anglo-Saxon foundations.

Sopley Church Mainly 13th-century building with a fine Jacobean pulpit. **Tyrrell's Ford** 2m N of Sopley. Region across which Sir Walter Tyrrell fled after the death of William Rufus.

Stoney Cross. Ocknell Clump Attractive spot where the New Forest's first plantation of Scots pine was introduced in 1775.

Entertainment

The only cinema in the district is at Holbury, therefore most of the district's entertainment is provided by amateur groups. Drama and operatic societies stage shows of high quality in the towns and at village halls. Dances are also held regularly at halls and hotels, while band concerts are staged at Barton-on-Sea and Milford-on-Sea. For further information tel. (042 128) 2269 (summer only) or 3121.

Shopping

Markets Lymington (Sat), Ringwood (Wed). Early Closing: Lymington and Lyndhurst (Wed), Ringwood and Fordingbridge (Mon & Thu).

Sport

Bowls. Lymington Public sports ground at Avenue Road. Open Apr–Sep 2pm–dusk. **Milford-on-Sea** Public green at Hurst Road. Open Apr–Sep daily. **New Milton** Recreation ground at Whitefield Road. Three public rinks. Open May–Sep 10.30–dusk. **Ringwood** Carvers Sports Ground. One public rink. Open Apr–Sep 2pm–dusk.

Cricket. Local pitches include Blackfield, Brockenhurst, Burley, Lymington (Southampton Road), Lyndhurst (Swan Green), New Milton (Ashley Sports Ground) and Pennington.

Indoor Sports. Centres at **New Milton** Arnewood Sports Centre, Gore Road. Facilities include swimming, squash, table-tennis and badminton *tel.* (0425) 617441. **Ringwood** Ringwood Recreation Centre, Parsonage Barn Lane. Facilities for squash, table tennis, netball, swimming and five-a-side football. Bar and cafeteria *tel.* (042 54) 78014.

Swimming. Coastal swimming can be enjoyed at the following places: Barton-on-Sea, Calshot, Lepe and Milford-on-Sea. Lymington has an open-air sea-water swimming pool of considerable size which stages an annual gala and regular water-polo matches.

Tennis. Lymington Lymington Sports Ground at Avenue Road. Four hard courts available throughout the year. Woodside Gardens has two courts also. **Lyndhurst** Lyndhurst Lawn Tennis Club at Sandy Lane. Three hard courts open until 6pm weekdays. **New Milton** Recreation Ground at Whitefield Road. Two all-weather and two shale courts. Available Apr–Oct 10.30–Dusk. **Ringwood** Carvers Sports Ground. Three grass courts (summer only) and one hard court. Open 9–dusk.

A cricket match outside the Balmer Lawn Hotel, near Brockenhurst

For the disabled

There are several designated spots in the New Forest catering specifically for the disabled.

Castle Hill South of Wood Green. Scenic views of the River Avon. Small parking area and seats.

Hatchet Pond West of Beaulieu off B3055. Fishing and picnicking area with ample parking space, toilets and rest points.

Wilverley Off Brockenhurst to Holmsley Road. Woodland and open forest including a special walk for the disabled. Good parking, toilets, rest points and picnic places.

Atlas

Key to Walks

① Godshill Area Walk   ② Fritham Area Walk   ③ Rufus Stone Walk

④ Linford Walk   ⑤ Knightwood Oak Walk   ⑥ Bolton's Bench Walk

⑦ King's Hat Walk   ⑧ Smugglers' Road Walk   ⑨ Wilverley Inclosure Walk

⑩ Ober Water Walk   ⑪ Beaulieu Heath Walk   ⑫ King's Copse Walk

⑬ Norley Moor Walk   ⑭ Beaulieu to Bucklers Hard Walk

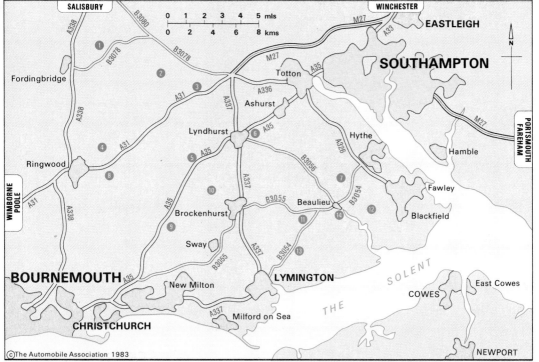

Warning: *The Forest can be very wet underfoot, even in the height of summer, and all walkers are strongly advised to wear stout walking shoes or boots. In winter or wet weather, progress in some parts (particularly the valleys and wet heaths) can be extremely difficult. We recommend that walkers should carry a 'Silva' type compass.*

Atlas Legend

VEGETATION

Limits of vegetation are defined by positioning of the symbols but may be delineated also by pecks or dots

	Coniferous trees
	Non-coniferous trees
	Mixed trees
	Coppice
	Orchard
	Scrub
	Bracken Rough grassland
	Heath
	Reeds
	Marsh
	Saltings

GRID REFERENCE SYSTEM

The map references used in this book are based on the Ordnance Survey National Grid, correct to within 100 metres. They comprise two letters and four figures, and are preceded by the atlas page number.
Thus the reference for Brockenhurst appears 10SU3002

10 is the atlas page number

SU identifies the major (100km) grid square concerned (see diagram)

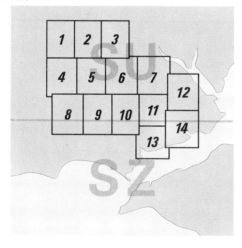

3002 locates the lower left-hand corner of the kilometre grid square in which Brockenhurst appears.

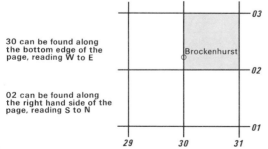

30 can be found along the bottom edge of the page, reading W to E

02 can be found along the right hand side of the page, reading S to N

GENERAL FEATURES

Church or Chapel	with tower
	with spire
	without tower or spire
	Glasshouse
	Lighthouse, lightship, beacon
VILLA	Roman antiquity (AD43 to AD420)
Castle	Other antiquities
	Site of antiquity
1066	Site of battle (with date)
pylons / poles	Electricity transmission line
	Gravel pit
	Sand pit
	Chalk pit, clay pit, or quarry
	Refuse or slag heap
	Sloping masonry
	Water
	Sand and shingle
	Mud
	Triangulation station
	Triangulation point on church, chapel, lighthouse, beacon, building, chimney
BP, BS	Boundary Post, Stone
T, A, R	Telephone Public, AA, RAC
MP, MS	Mile Post, Stone
W, Spr	Well, Spring
NT	National Trust always open
FC	Forestry Commission Area Pedestrians only (observe local signs)

ROADS AND PATHS
Not necessarily rights of way

M27	Motorway
A 36(T)	Trunk road
A 336	Main road
B 3074	Secondary road
A 336	Dual carriageway
	Road generally over 4m wide
	Road generally under 4m wide
	Drive or track
	Path
◆ ◆ ◆	Waymarked path
Solent Way	Named path

Unfenced roads and tracks are shown by pecked lines

PUBLIC RIGHTS OF WAY
Public rights of way shown on this Atlas may not be evident on the ground

- - - - - - Footpath	Public Paths
- - - - Bridleway	
+++++	By-way open to all traffic
⊥⊤⊥⊤⊥	Road used as a public path

Public rights of way indicated have been derived from Definitive Maps as amended by later enactments or instruments held by Ordnance Survey on 1st December 1982 and are shown subject to the limitations imposed by the scale of mapping.

The representation in this atlas of any other road track or path is no evidence of the existence of a right of way.

RAILWAYS

———— Multiple track	Standard gauge
- - - - Single track	
....	Narrow gauge
	Siding
	Level Crossing
	Station
	Cutting
	Embankment
	Tunnel
	Road over and under

HEIGHTS AND ROCK FEATURES

50	Determined	ground survey
285	by	air survey

Surface heights are to the nearest metre above mean sea level. Heights shown close to a triangulation pillar refer to the station height at ground level and not necessarily to the summit.

Vertical face

Boulders

Contours are shown at 5 metres vertical interval

TOURIST AND LEISURE INFORMATION
RENSEIGNEMENTS CONCERNANT LE TOURISME ET LES ACTIVITÉS DE LOISIR

TOURISTEN-INFORMATION UND FREIZEIT-AUSKUNFT

⋏ Camp site
Terrain de camping
Campingplatz

🚐 Caravan site
Terrain pour caravanes
Wohnwagenplatz

P Parking
Parking
Parkplatz

ℹ Information Centre
Bureau d' information
Informationsbüro

▲ Youth hostel
Auberge de jeunesse
Jugendherberge

☎ T Public Telephone
Téléphone publique
Telefon, öffentlich

☎ A R AA and RAC Telephones
Téléphone, AA/RAC
Telefon, Automobilklub

🚌 Bus or coach station
Gare d'autobus ou d'autocar
Busbahnhof

✕ Picnic site
Emplacement de pique-nique
Picknickplatz

⌐ Golf course or links
Terrain de golf
Golfplatz

Priory / MUSEUM — Selected places of interest
Endroits d'un intérêt particulier
Ausgewählte Sehenswürdig – keiten

☀ Viewpoint
Point de vue
Aussichtspunkt

PC Public convenience (rural areas)
WC (à la campagne)
Toiletten in ländlichen Gebieten

U Riding establishment
Manège
Reitanstalt

⇌ Railway Station
Gare de Chemins de fer
Bahnhof

WALKS
SENTIERS RECOMMANDES
EMPFOHLENE WANDERWEGE

← Route for walkers
Sentier Signalisé
markierter Wanderweg

 New Forest boundary
Limite du New Forest
Grenze des New Forest

Routes to the
New Forest

168 Shrewsbury
172 Welshpool
158 Telford
BIR
174 Newtown
Bridgnorth 147
133 Kidderminster
A44 179 Llangurig
Aberystwyth 203
Ludlow 140
170 Rhayader
129 Leominster
117 Worcester
New Quay 204
156 Builth Wells
124 Hereford
164 Llandovery
143 Brecon
110 Ross-on-Wye
Gloucester 93
Abergavenny 122
137 Merthyr Tydfil
90 Chepstow
165 SWANSEA
Severn Bridge TOLL
125 Pontypridd
103 Newport
24
71 BRISTOL
CARDIFF 118
Chippenham 55
Bath 58
Bristol *Channel*
Warminster 40
85 Bridgwater
139 Barnstaple
Taunton 90
59 Yeovil
34 Blandford Forum
84 Honiton
100 EXETER
126 Okehampton
62 Bridport
BOURN 2
Dorchester 47
Launceston 146
55 Weymouth
143 PLYMOUTH

N

0   5   10   15   20 mls
0   10   20   30 kms

Stamford
173

150
LEICESTER

169
PETERBOROUGH

137
MINGHAM

126
COVENTRY

132
Market
Harborough

131
Kettering

149
Huntingdon

144
CAMBRIDGE

115
NORTHAMPTON

Stratford-
upon-Avon
114

Banbury
98

128
Bedford

108
Luton

114
Stevenage

90
Cheltenham

96
Aylesbury

99
St Albans

75
OXFORD

78
High
Wycombe

74
Cirencester

86
LONDON

59
SWINDON

58
READING

74
Slough

103
Tunbridge
Wells

48
Marlborough

47
Newbury

71
Staines

72
Dorking

78
Reigate

44
Devizes

41
Basingstoke

48
Farnham

59
Guildford

100
Sevenoaks

81
Crawley

90
East
Grinstead

Salisbury
19

22
Winchester

73
Horsham

83
Haywards Heath

41
Petersfield

57
Petworth

9
SOUTHAMPTON

70
BRIGHTON

15
Ringwood

**NEW
FOREST**
Lyndhurst

41
Chichester

61
Worthing

MOUTH

8
Lymington

PORTSMOUTH
30

Yarmouth
Isle of Wight

ENGLISH   CHANNEL

Extent of Key Map

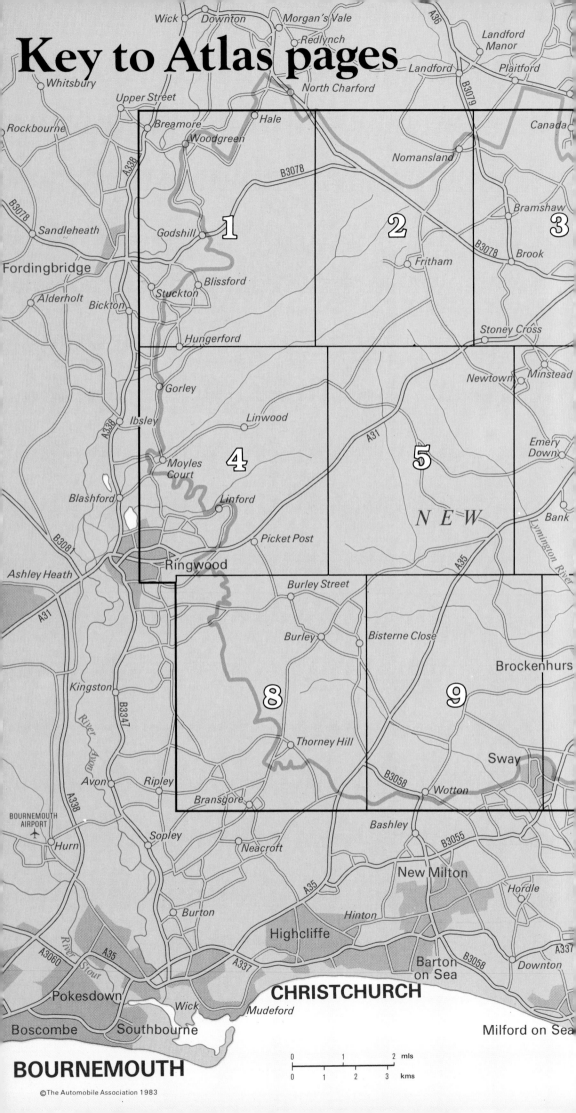

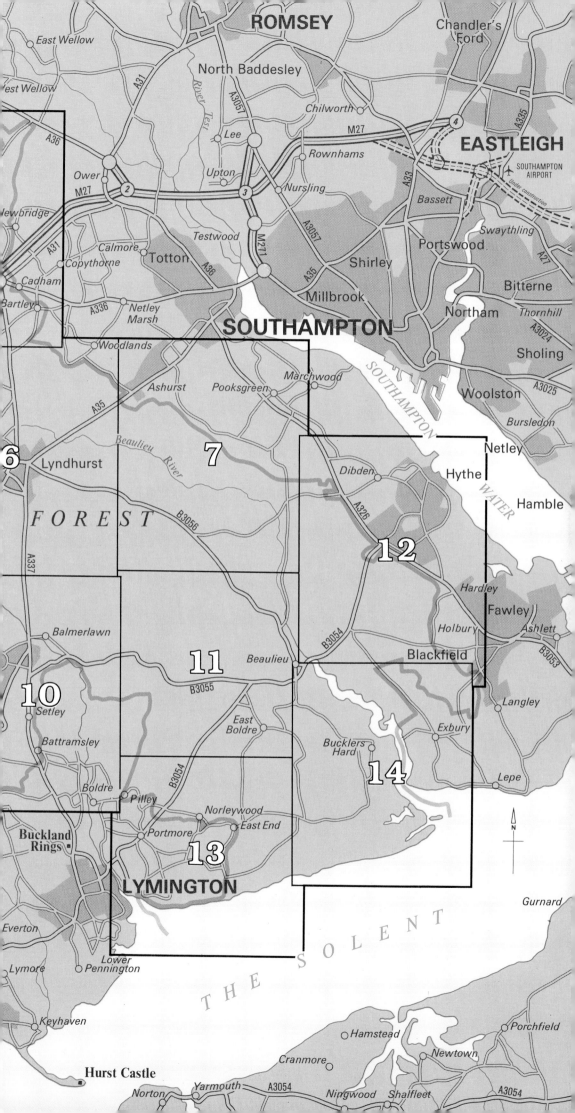

Godshill Area Walk

Allow 90 minutes

A walk through a forestry inclosure with a tremendous variety of broad-leaved and coniferous trees. The latter part of the walk gives lovely views across the Avon valley. Easy going along gravelled tracks and metalled roads.

At the far end of the car park a forestry gate leads off to the left into the trees. Go through this gate and walk on until the path meets a gravel track, and turn right. This part of Godshill Inclosure has a quite remarkable diversity of trees in it. There are conifers of all ages, shapes and sizes, as well as oak, sweet chestnut and rowan scattered about in a haphazard fashion.

Reach a crossways at a wide junction and turn left, following the gravel path slightly downhill. Among the plants growing beside the path along this part of the walk is broom, whose yellow flowers brighten the glades in midsummer.

Where the gravelled path veers off to the right by a stand of fine oak trees, take a little green path that goes off to the left. This path leads through an area of large oak trees under which grows holly. In spring a profusion of wild flowers grows beneath these trees.

Reach a Forest gate, go through it and turn right on to a metalled road. Shortly turn left up a metalled road which is signposted to Castle Hill. Reach a small gravelled parking area. From here there are magnificent views across the Avon valley.

Follow the road down through woodland to a group of buildings. Just before the houses, follow a path which leads off to the right between a row of wooden posts set in the ground. This leads up to the earthworks on Castle Hill, the site of an Iron Age fort which once commanded the whole of this part of the valley.

Return to the roadway and pass through a small forestry gate which leads back into Godshill Inclosure. Follow the path as it leads away to the left, going quite steeply uphill. Once more the walk leads through a mixture of oak, beech and chestnut, with a really dark conifer plantation away to the left. Among the wild flowers along the woodland verge is enchanter's nightshade, a small plant with delicate white flowers that was used as a protection against spells cast by elves.

Take the second path on the left. Shortly this becomes a gravelled track. Reach a Forest gate, cross the road from Woodgreen to Godshill and enter another Forest gate. Reach the junction where the walk was started, and turn right to return to the car park.

Enchanter's nightshade

Fritham Area Walk

Allow 40 minutes

This walk leads along gravelled tracks and woodland rides among the trees of Queen North Wood and across the wide expanse of Fritham Plain. Easy going for the most part along clear tracks.

Start from the car park at Fritham. At the entrance to the car park is a black metal post box, erected before 1900 by the Schultz gunpowder factory (which was situated at Eyeworth) to make the postman's journey easier.

From the post box turn right along the metalled road towards the Royal Oak Inn. Pigs can often be seen rooting about on the open area here and in the surrounding woodlands. These belong to local residents, who are allowed to let their pigs roam free by ancient right of pannage. The pigs find most to eat in autumn, when the ground is littered with beechmast and acorns.

Just before the inn turn right along a gravelled track, with houses on the left. Among the houses is a handsome little chapel, built for the Free United Church in 1904. There are views away to the left across a green valley towards the scatterings of buildings which make up Fritham village.

At the end of the gravelled track reach a Forest gate and veer right across the open space. Turn to the left, cross a gulley, and then branch right, following a woodland ride up through the trees of Queen North Wood. This wood is composed chiefly of oak and beech, with holly growing between. It is a good bird watching spot, especially for finches and members of the tit family.

Beyond a particularly huge and gnarled oak tree emerge on to the open expanse of Fritham Plain. Keep straight on across the heath and shortly reach Green Pond. This is a shallow area of water set among short grass. The short turf is often visited by green woodpeckers, who probe the soil in search of invertebrates.

Continue ahead on the broad track and after a short distance reach a gravelled Forest road. Turn right on to it. The open character of Fritham Plain soon changes, and a dense growth of holly stretches away to left and right. Through this foliage Eyeworth Lodge can be glimpsed away to the left.

Return to the car park.

Holly blossom and bush

◁ MAP 2

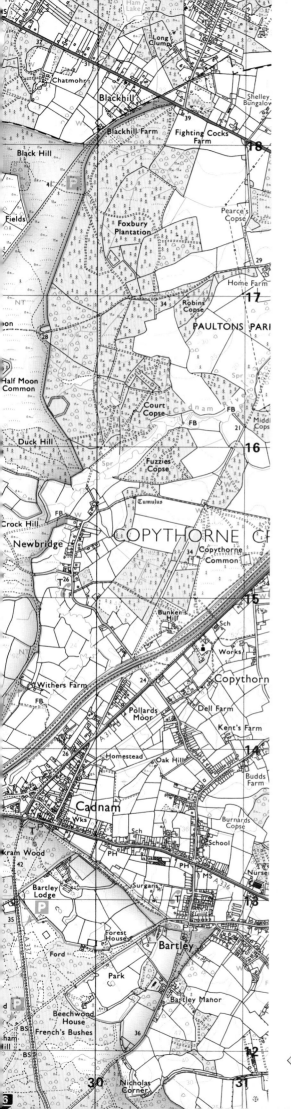

Rufus Stone Walk

Allow 60 minutes

A walk across heathland and through lovely mixed woodland. Easy going for the most part, but wet underfoot. Some of the paths across the heathland are not well defined.

Start the walk from the Rufus Stone car park which is opposite the Rufus Stone. From the car park, cross the road to the Rufus Stone, then walk up the road towards the A31. Take the track which leads off to the right and into a small clump of trees. On the other side of the trees, follow the winding track until it emerges onto heathland. The busy main road is away to the left but marvellous views open up to the right, across the treetops and out of the Forest.
   Continue along a wide track through the heathland with a white house in the distance. Shortly before you reach the white house you will see a red bungalow on the other side of the road. Turn off the track through a clump of holly. Shortly come out on to an open area with trees directly in front of you. Head for the trees and follow a path downhill with the trees directly on the right. The path now enters an area of lovely old woodland, with oak, beech and holly.
   Reach a stream and turn slightly to the right, following the path that runs parallel with it. After a little while enter an open area, and on its far side reach a well-used track and turn right. Follow the path. The edge of Blackthorn Copse is on your left and there is an open area stretching away to the right. In summer flycatchers are likely to be seen on this part of the walk. These little summer-visiting birds perch on branches and fence posts, and fly into the open areas to catch flies. This they do in a swirl of clapping wings.
   Shortly you will see the Walter Tyrrell pub in front of you. Complete the walk either by returning along the road to the Rufus Stone car park, or by following the numerous paths which lead beside and through the woodland alongside the road.

Spotted flycatchers

MAP 3

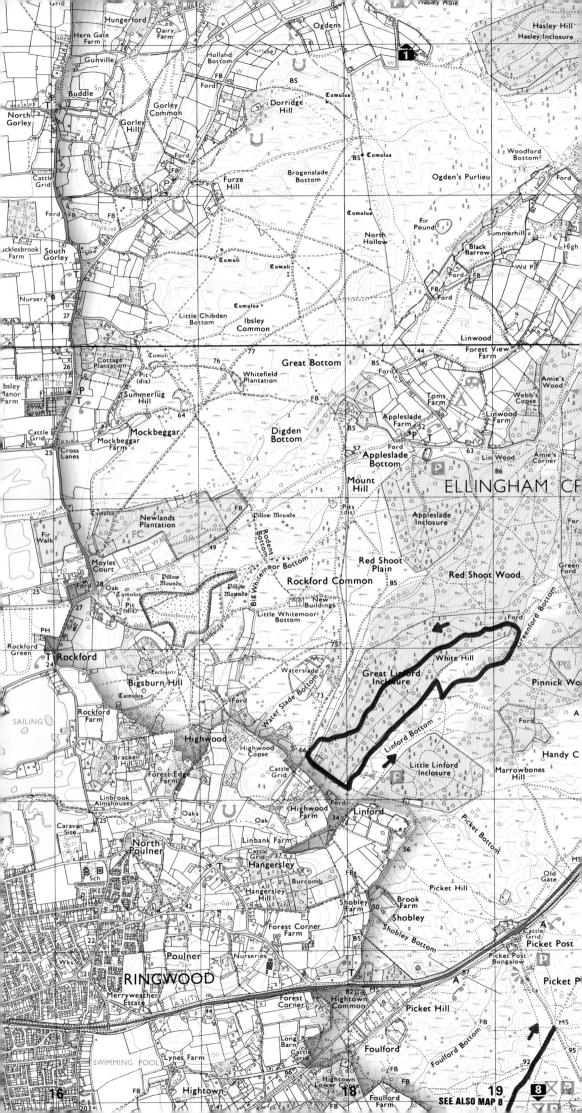

Linford Walk

Allow 90 minutes

This walk follows the course of one of the Forest's most delightful streams and then takes a path through an inclosure which has both coniferous and deciduous trees. Easy going along well-defined paths.

From Linford Bottom car park follow a forestry track beside Great Linford Inclosure, and then turn right to reach a bridge over Linford Brook. Turn left and follow the brook upstream. Moss- and lichen-covered oaks, willows and blackthorns line the banks of the stream. Some of the oaks have fallen, and in these hornets may have made their nests. Largest of British wasps, hornets can be distinguished by their brown and orange markings and disturbingly loud buzzing hum. They are rare insects, only commonly seen in the woodlands of southern England. Despite their frightening reputation and formidable appearance, hornets rarely sting people.

Emerge from the trees beside the stream and turn left on to a gravelled forestry path. Reach a Forest gate and enter Great Linford Inclosure. Follow the gravelled track through the Inclosure. Planted with stands of oak and conifers, Great Linford was inclosed in 1846, and many of its trees have reached maturity. Those who walk quietly will probably see fallow deer in the Inclosure. These enchanting creatures were probably introduced to Britain by the Normans, and since that time they have been an essential part of the Forest scene.

Leave the Inclosure by a Forest gate and walk up through bracken to reach a metalled road. Turn left, go past a Forest Keeper's house and return to the car park.

Hornets

MAP 4

Knightwood Oak Walk

Allow 20 minutes

This walk follows a short way-marked trail in the area of the Knightwood Oak – possibly the most famous tree in the Forest. Easy going along well-defined tracks.

From the Knightwood Oak car park a gravelled track marked with yellow posts leads past several features of interest in the vicinity of the Knightwood Oak. The Knightwood Oak itself is one of the largest and oldest trees in the Forest. Its many-branched crown reveals that it was once pollarded, and this probably explains the tree's great age, since pollarding can prolong the life of a tree almost indefinitely.

Bear left at the Knightwood Oak Inclosure, following the gravelled path. Cross two little bridges over ditches and turn right to follow the line of a Forest fence. Beyond this fence is an open area which is one of many animal pounds scattered through the Forest. Ponies and cattle are corralled here once a year to be branded and tail-marked.

Turn right by an information panel explaining the pound and reach the exposed roots of a felled beech tree. An information panel here explains that the tree died as the result of the severe drought of 1976.

Pass the Knightwood Oak once more and bear left along the path. On the right is one of the most fascinating sights in the Forest. Two trees, an oak and a beech, have grown up fused together in an embrace known botanically as enosculation. This is most unusual with different species of trees but relatively common when the trees are of the same species. A little further on is an oak planted by Her Majesty the Queen in 1979 to mark the ninth centenary of the New Forest.

Return to the car park.

Knightwood Oak

◁ MAP 5

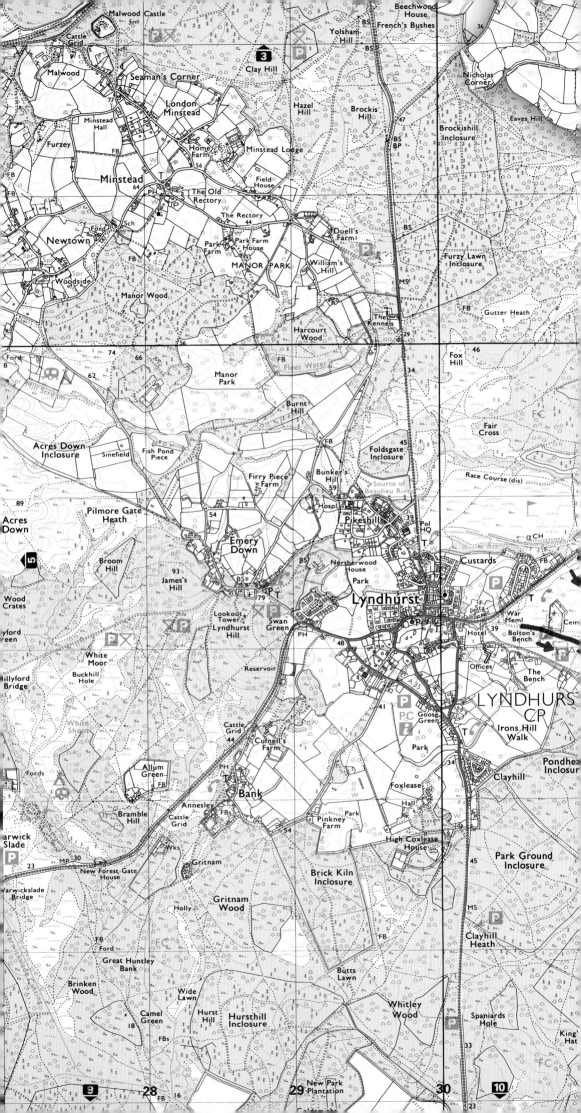

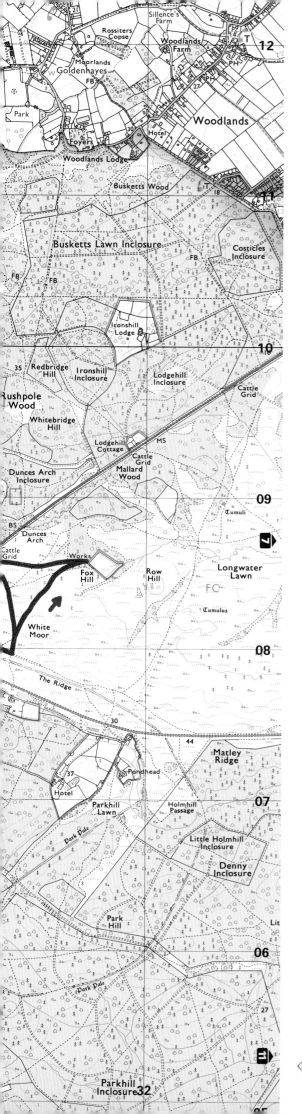

Bolton's Bench Walk

Allow 60 minutes

A walk across heathland; easy going for the most part, and starting from the car park at Bolton's Bench, which was opened by Her Majesty the Queen.

Follow a wide, clear path with a cemetery on the left. This is an exceptionally popular spot in summer, but within minutes the crowds drop away and excellent views of the heathlands and distant woodlands open up.

Take the first clear white track to the left. You will pass through an area that was burned off at some point in the past – the bare, black branches of gorse rise out of the young heather and grass. This is an indication of the way in which the Forest's heathlands are kept open, for by nature they would soon become woodland. The heaths are burned off at regular intervals, which kills trees and gorse bushes, but the tough roots and seeds of the heather are not destroyed, and new shoots rapidly grow up, providing tender young food for the Forest's grazing animals. A little further on a number of rowans or mountain ashes will be seen growing among the heath and gorse. These lovely trees, their bright red berries a delight in summer, probably grew from berries which had been eaten by birds. Gulleys on either side of the track reveal the poorer nature of the Forest's heathland soils – gravelly and leached.

Shortly enter an area of self-sown Scots pine. This small area is almost like a natural pine wood – the trees are of all sizes and ages, and their shapes vary from conical, to spreading, to flat topped. Some are close together, some are widely scattered.

Emerge, just beyond a large Scots pine, into an open area which is bordered on the right by a holly hedge. Retrace your steps to a small clearing, with a clump of large Scots pine on the right. Take the path running parallel with your original path. (It is rather overgrown with young pines but it is passable.) Emerge on to heather, with a row of trees away to the right. Keep slightly to the left and enter a small clump of birch and pine. A path leads out across the heather towards the main road into Lyndhurst. The tower of Lyndhurst church can be clearly seen in front and to the left.

Reach a cattle underpass under the road and turn left back into the heather. Shortly, on the right, pass a small pond. Keep straight on for a while, then reach a crossroads of tracks among gorse and keep ahead on a well-defined track. Continue through heather and eventually return to the wide track; then turn right to return to the car park.

New Forest Pony

MAP 6

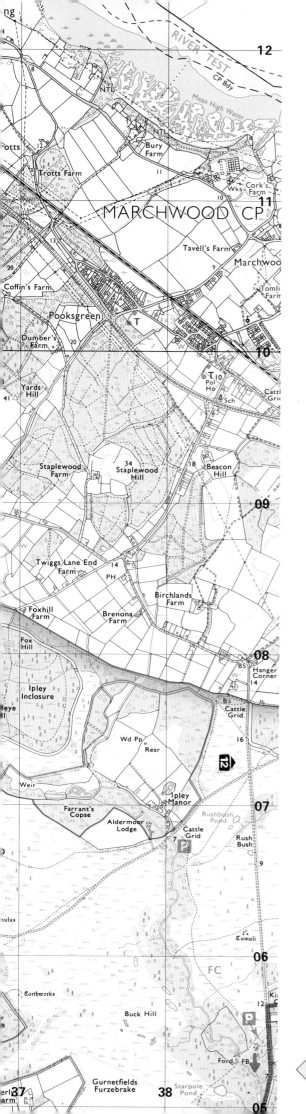

King's Hat Walk

Allow 40 minutes

A walk through mixed woodlands and across an area of typical New Forest heathland. Easy going along gravelled forestry tracks.

From North Gate car park turn left on to the metalled by-road, and after approximately 150 yards turn right through a gate to join a gravelled forest track. This track leads through Foxhunting Inclosure. At first the walk passes through stands of Scots pines, but beyond a junction there is an area of beech and oak with an understorey of holly, rhododendron and sweet chestnut to the right of the track. Shortly the woodland becomes deciduous on both sides and then becomes coniferous once more, with a scattering of birch.

   Reach a gate and pass through it to enter Crabhat Inclosure. On the left is a small animal pound. Beyond the gate the character of the walk changes once more, with well-grown pines on the left and an open area planted with young trees on the right.

   Shortly the path turns sharp left to follow the edge of Crabhat Inclosure. Away to the right, across the heathland, are the woodlands of Dibden Inclosure. Behind these are the housing estates and industrial complexes that line the banks of Southampton Water.

   Cross an area of open heathland and then go through a gate to enter King's Hat Inclosure. At first this is composed of oak with an understorey of holly and young conifers, but beyond a little brook be-decked with ferns of several sorts there are thick ranks of conifers.

   Reach a junction and turn left. Shortly a Forest Keeper's house can be seen through the trees on the left. Keep ahead and emerge on to the by-road. Turn left to return to the car park.

The walk shown on this map continues on Map 12, and is the Forestry Commission's preferred walk for this area.

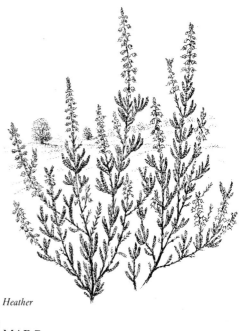

Heather

◁ MAP 7

Smugglers' Road Walk

Allow 60 minutes

A walk across Forest heathland and along the famous Smugglers' Road. Easy going along a wide track.

From the Smugglers' Road car park walk along the minor road towards Knaves Ash. Reach a track which leads off right on to the heath. Go uphill and emerge on to the Smugglers' Road. The famous Smugglers' Road is an ancient ridgeway which gives superb views in all directions. To the west it looks across the Avon valley (hidden by intervening hills) to the wooded slopes beyond Ringwood. To the south-east, on the other side of Vales Moor, the earthworks of Castle Hill can be clearly seen. This ancient path was used by smugglers landing at Christchurch harbour in order to transport their illicit stores of tea, 'baccy or rum safely to Southampton. Legend has it that they were assisted by a local woman called Lovey Warne. If there were any Revenue men too near for comfort she would stand on Verely Hill wearing a scarlet cloak, thus warning the smugglers not to come out of hiding. Away to the west the heath drops down towards the Forest boundary. The higher parts of the heath are covered in bell heather and gorse, but heather will not grow in wet areas, so in the lower, wetter parts of the heath it is replaced by cross-leaved heath and various rushes and grasses. Deer can sometimes be seen in this area; they tend to feed in the woodland edge along the boundary. Fortunate walkers may see red deer here. These magnificent creatures, the largest wild animals in Britain, are few in number in the New Forest and are therefore rarely seen.

The Smugglers' Road track can be followed all the way to the minor road which crosses Picket Plain. Walkers can turn back at any point to return to the car park.

The walk shown on this map continues on Map 4, and is the Forestry Commission's preferred walk for this area.

Red deer stag

MAP 8

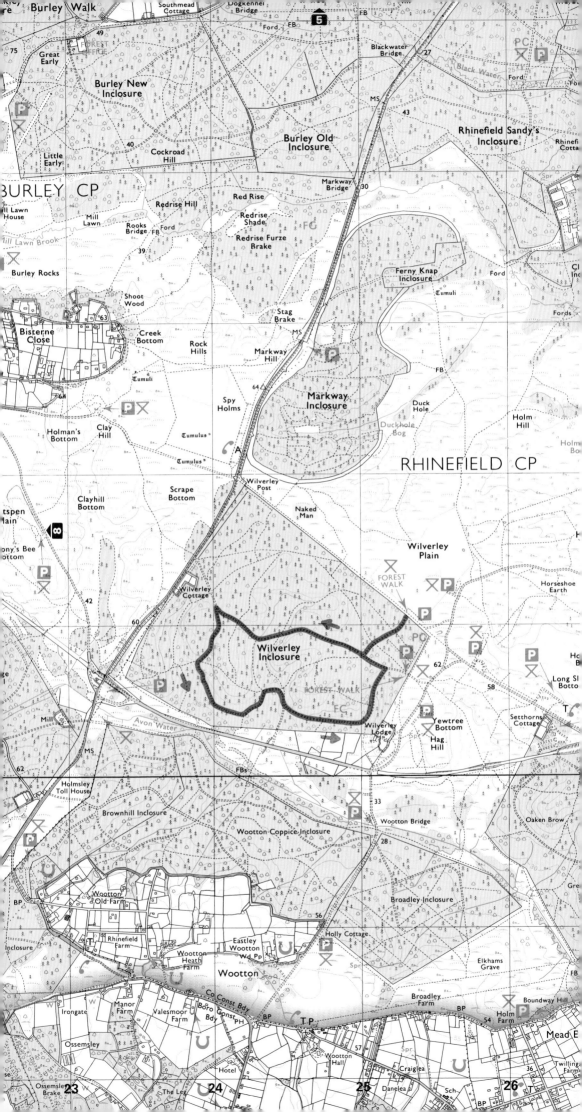

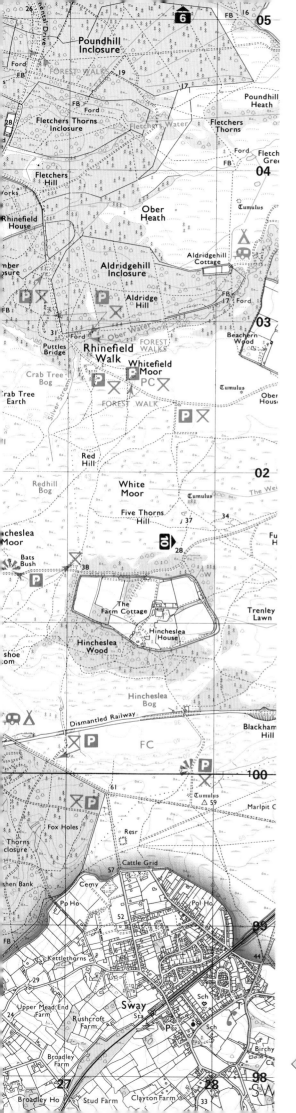

Wilverley Inclosure Walk

Allow 90 minutes

A walk through the mixed woodlands of Wilverley Inclosure. The paths are easy going, and way-marked. Those walking from Wilverley Plain car park should follow the green posts. Yellow posts mark the round trip from Wilverley Inclosure car park. Wilverley was orginally inclosed in 1775, but the planting made at that time failed, and a new planting was made in 1809. The strip of oak which runs along the edge of the Inclosure on either side of the car park dates from that time. The Inclosure was thrown open in 1846, and fenced once more in 1896.

From the car park at Wilverley Plain enter the Inclosure through a gate and walk straight along a gravelled path. Shortly a path on the left leads along Wilverley Stroll – a short way-marked trail specially set out for disabled persons. Keep forward on the main walk. On either side of the path dark plantations stretch away into the distance. The trees cast such dense shade that nothing grows on the needle-strewn forest floor. Shortly, the character of the woodland changes, with widely-spaced trees standing among a rich and diverse ground flora.

Turn right at a T-junction. An information panel on the left explains that trees are harvested mainly in the winter to avoid disturbing birds and other creatures. The walk now enters an area where there is a mixture of broad-leaved trees. Among them are birch, beech, and several very large oaks and sweet chestnuts. Next, on the right, is a stand of large firs, with self-sown seedlings growing beneath them.

Turn sharp left, following the green marker posts. In front of a partially-cleared area on the right an information panel explains that the trees which stood in this area – Scots pine and European larch – were felled when they reached maturity at about 80 years old. These trees have now been replaced with a new planting of Corsican pine.

Go down hill and enter an area dominated by a number of ancient oaks. From a natural history point of view oaks are among the most valuable of British trees, since they support a far greater variety of wildlife than any other British species. Many hundreds of different species of invertebrates may be found living on an oak, and these attract birds like tits, nuthatches and tree creepers.

Reach a junction and turn left, going uphill. The walk now passes stands of trees in which a great variety of coniferous species are represented.

Reach a T-junction. The right turn leads to Wilverley Inclosure car park, and the left turn leads eventually back to the car park on Wilverley Plain.

Marsh tit

MAP 9

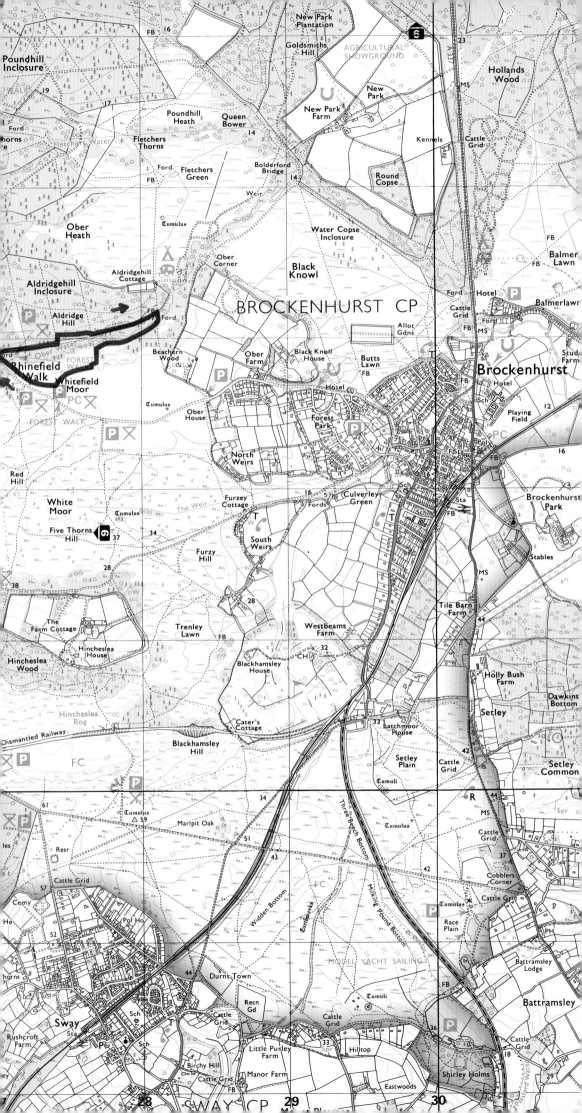

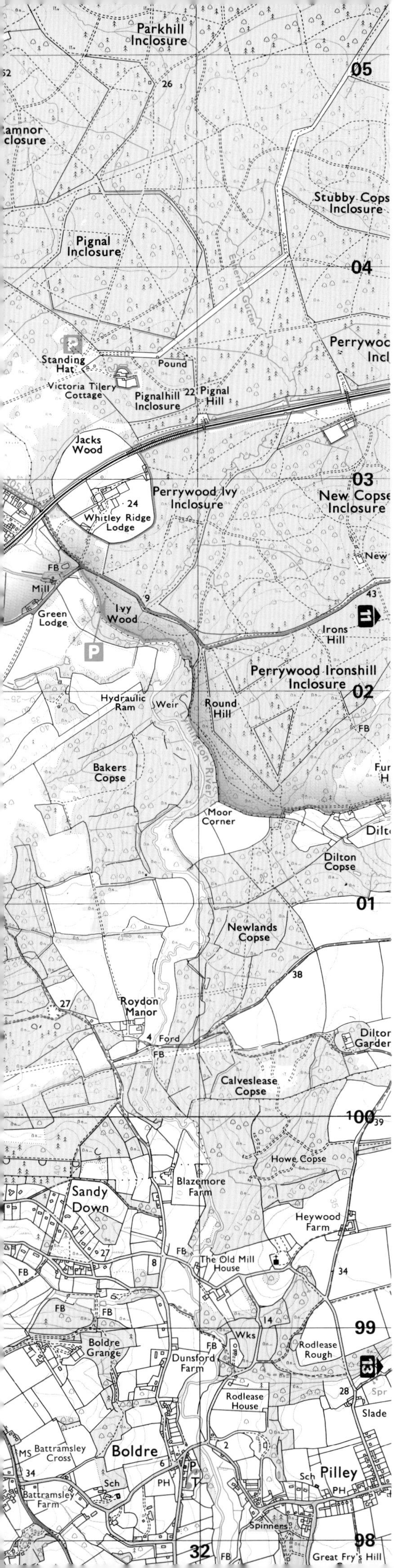

Ober Water Walk

Allow 30 or 50 minutes

This is a Forestry Commission way-marked trail and it begins from the car park at Puttles Bridge. The path is clearly marked, well laid out and easy to follow. Red marker posts take you on a long walk, which takes about 50 minutes, and yellow markers take you on a shorter walk of about 30 minutes.

Walk out of the car park through an area of Scots pine. Introduced to the Forest in 1776, Scots pine has spread over large areas of open heathland by natural regeneration. A little further along is a dead pine that would normally be removed to keep the Forest hygenic. It has been left to show that such dead trees are valuable habitats for a number of creatures. It is pock-marked with oval holes made by longhorn beetles as they emerged from underneath the bark where they had spent their larval stage.

Enter an area where there are more broad-leaved trees. Several large beeches covered with lichens and mosses can be seen here – a sure sign that the air is unpolluted. The walk divides shortly afterwards.

Take either the shorter, yellow-marked path which crosses the Ober Water or the longer, red-marked path which branches to the left. The longer walk now leads through an avenue of ancient, twisted oak trees, covered in lichens and mosses. Many of these trees were once coppiced – hence their distorted shapes. All the woodland on the left is part of the Aldridge-hill Inclosure, which was first inclosed in 1775. The oaks which had been planted at that time were felled in World War I, and the oaks seen today have grown from old coppice stools and seedlings.

Reach the next information pillar, in front of a number of stunted beech trees. This explains that these trees would naturally grow up in this glade, but are prevented from doing so by the grazing activity of fallow deer.

Cross the Ober Water by a footbridge. The water is stained brown by peat, and the minerals which are in it. In high summer the water is continually disturbed by thousands of little insects called pond skaters, which are able to 'walk on the water' by making use of the surface tension of the water.

Follow the Ober Water back towards the car park. The Ober Water twists and turns in a slow and lazy fashion, and in parts Ox-bow lakes have formed.

Bear left with the path. Moving away from the stream, the path crosses a wet area, dotted with pines, to reach an area of short grass. This was ploughed for crops in World War II and is now kept as grassland by the Forestry Commission for the benefit of commoners' animals.

Enter a car park on Whitefield Moor and descend. The way-marked path now runs parallel with the road and descends into a very wet area, although the path itself is raised and dry. This area is so acid and wet that trees find great difficulty in growing. The Scots pines that do stand here look like seedlings, but in fact they are between 30 and 40 years old.

Return to the Puttles Bridge car park via a footbridge across the Ober Water.

MAP 10

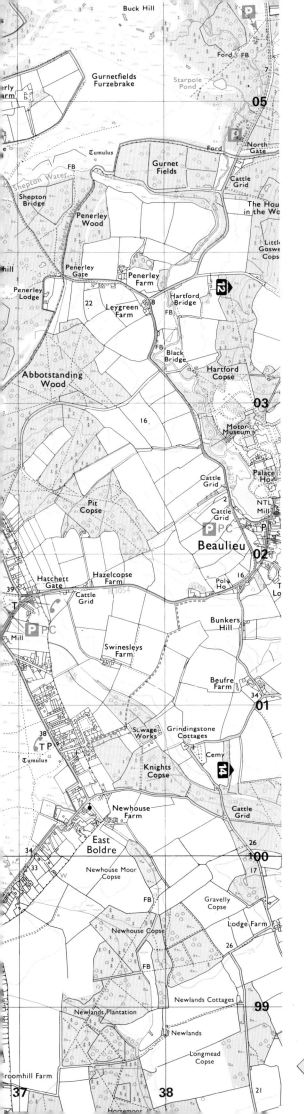

Beaulieu Heath Walk

Allow 40 minutes

A walk across open heathland over the site of a dismantled airfield. There are good views in all directions, especially towards the Isle of Wight. Easy going along metalled tracks and well defined paths.

Park at the Beaulieu Heath car park and walk in a clockwise direction round the perimeter track of the old airfield. The airfield was constructed in 1942, and from here many operations were launched during the last years of World War II. It continued in use until 1959, when most of the runways were removed, but the open character of the area is maintained by the Forestry Commission. This part of Beaulieu Heath is comparatively dry, and is grazed by ponies and rabbits. Much of it is heather, but there are areas of well-cropped grass and many gorse bushes, as well as occasional willows, birches and Scots pine. The heather looks at its best in late summer, when the flowers blossom and colour the heath purple. Other wild plants may be found growing beneath the heather; these include the yellow flowers of tormentil and the white sprays of heath bedstraw.

Continue along the metalled track to a low gate. Walk past the gate and continue past an area of hard standing on the left. Shortly before the metalled track veers to the right, turn sharp right to follow the lines of the old runways. There are excellent views all round along this part of the walk. To the west can be seen the distant woodlands of the Forest, while to the north-east are the towers of the Fawley refinery and to the south-east are the hills of the Isle of Wight. Beaulieu Heath is dotted with tumuli, the burial mounds of Bronze Age people who eked a living from these thin soils some 4,000 years ago. The runway track passes the site of several of these tombs, but they are very difficult to pinpoint on the ground. Plants are trying to colonise the old runway, but the harsh ground conditions, and the continual grazing activities of ponies, cattle and rabbits prevent most from gaining a foothold. Various lichens and mosses flourish on the bare ground.

At the far end of the runway reach the perimeter track once more and return to the car park.

Tormentil

MAP 11

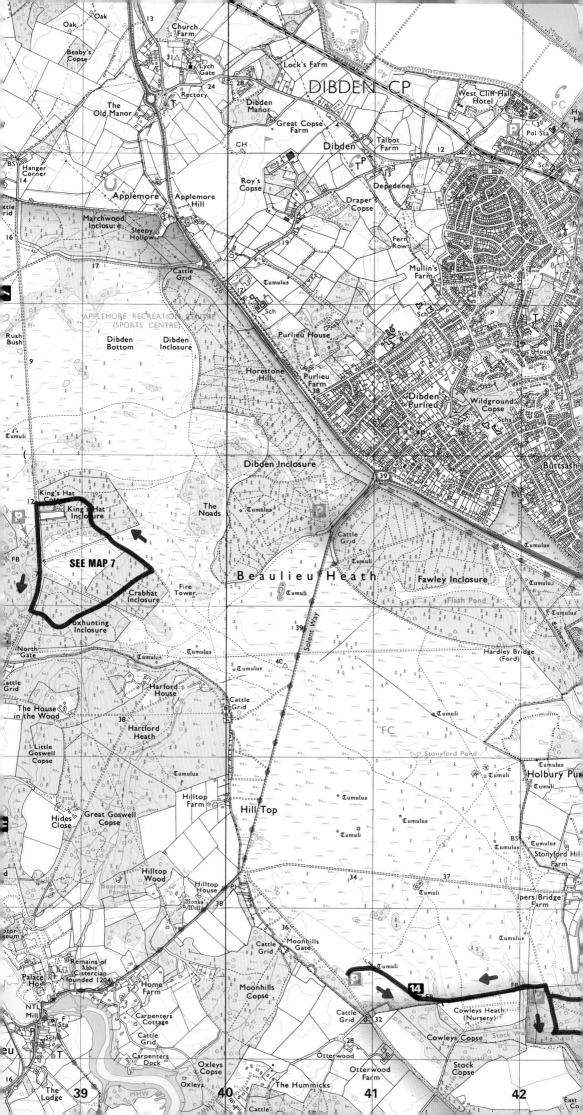

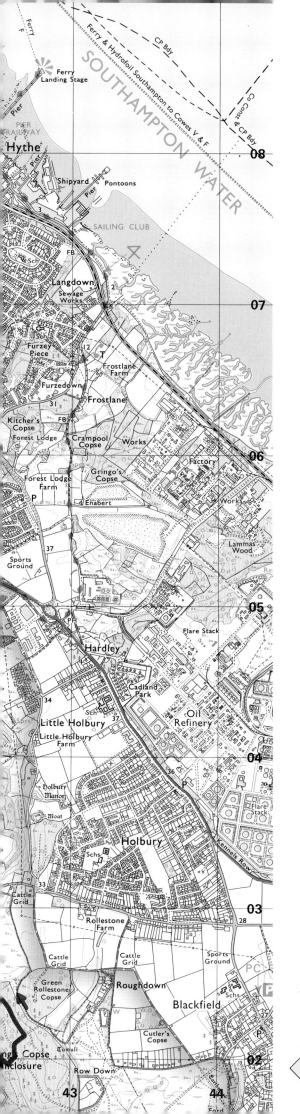

King's Copse Walk

Allow 60 minutes or 120 minutes

This walk can either be made from the car park at King's Copse Inclosure, or begun from the Moonhills car park. It will take about an hour to walk around the Inclosure and a further hour to make the complete journey to and from Moonhills.

From Moonhills follow a track across heathland passing the low hump of a tumulus, or burial mound, on the left. Follow the path which bears to the right and then enters a delightful strip of woodland at the edge of the Forest. On the other side of the Forest fence are the grounds of Cowleys Heath Nursery. Growing right on the Forest boundary are ancient pollarded oaks, their multiple stems contorted into strange shapes.

Cross two small footbridges on the way to King's Copse Inclosure. The little streams that flow under the footbridges have created tiny valley habitats where willow, birch, oak and holly cast dappled shades on waters that are patrolled by dragonflies and damselflies.

Reach the car park at King's Copse. Go through the Forest gate and almost immediately reach a three-way junction. Take the right-hand one. Go steeply downhill, and at the bottom of the hill cross the little Stock Water by a footbridge. Immediately past the footbridge turn left, with a stand of oak trees on the left. On the left there is a plantation of young Norway spruce, with other trees including young oak.

After a while reach a junction and keep left, with the plantation still on the left. On the right will be seen a large birch tree and several stately oaks. The track along here is wide and grassy, and in the exposed earth at its edge may be found the tracks of badgers and other creatures.

Reach another junction, with oak with an understorey of holly in front; turn left here and almost immediately cross the Stock Water again by another footbridge. Directly on the other side of the bridge turn left on to a gravel track. Just past the bridge there are a number of sweet chestnuts on the right.

Shortly reach another junction and turn right. Turn left at a junction, with a Forest gate a little way in front. For a while the ride goes through conifers and then begins to descend into mixed wood mainly composed of oak with an understorey of holly, bracken, brambles and ferns.

Bear left and descend to reach another footbridge. Once over the bridge start climbing up through conifers again. Eventually meet the ride along which the Inclosure walk was begun and turn right to return to the car park.

Badger

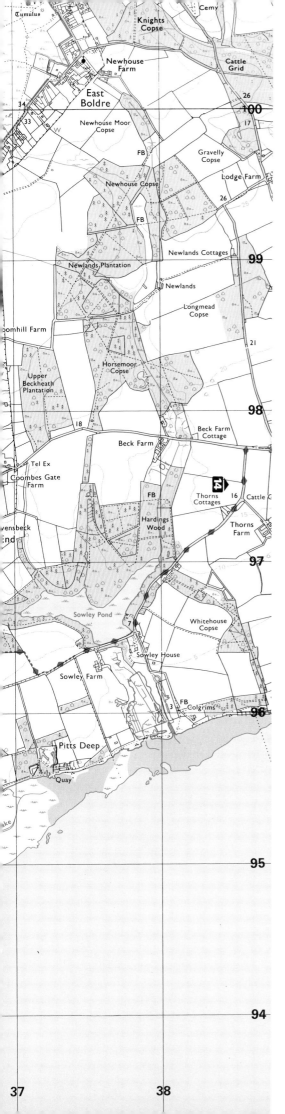

Norley Moor Walk

Allow 70 minutes

This walk begins at the Norley Moor car park and leads along fairly well-defined paths through areas of conifers and mixed deciduous woodlands.

At the north-east end of the car park, farthest from the entrance, turn right through a Forest gate. This gate (which you must close behind you) leads into Norley Inclosure, first enclosed in 1881.

Follow the path as it stretches clearly away into an area of mature conifers. Among the many birds that flit among these trees are likely to be tree creepers, which clamber up and down the trunks searching for insects in every nook and cranny. The trees here are widely spaced, allowing the sunlight to enter and encouraging a ground cover which includes heather, bracken and seedling trees.

Reach a junction of tracks and turn left. Along here you will probably see large piles of pine needles; these are the nests of wood ants. You may also see purposeful columns of wood ants – some leaving the nest and some carrying foodstuffs and building materials back to the nest. They keep to the same paths, which become quite worn by the tramp of millions of tiny feet.

Reach another junction and turn sharp right on to a gravelled path. On the left is a plantation of young conifers, with large birch, oak and Scots pine growing among them. Here, because there is still plenty of light, there is a thick ground cover of bramble, sedges, grasses and wild flowers. After a while on the right is a small clump of sweet chestnut. This species of tree was probably first introduced into this country by the Romans; it is found on light soils in southern England, where it was formerly coppiced. Shortly the character of the woodland ride changes again, with at first young beech trees on the left and then a mixture of oak and holly. Behind this screen of deciduous trees are dense ranks of conifers.

Reach another junction. On the left, beyond the Forest fence, are the open fields of Norley Farm.

Keep to the right on the gravelled track. After about 300 yards, by a solitary beech tree, turn sharp right down a grassy Forest path. On either side are thick ranks of conifers, with 'brash' (felled branches) littering the Forest floor beneath. The trees are grown close together so that they grow straight and tall with few branches that would cause knots in the wood. There is very little growing on the Forest floor beneath these trees, but along the ride there are flowers including fox gloves. Numerous wet hollows here support a variety of damp-loving plants.

Reach a boundary bank, cross it and enter an area of mature trees that have been thinned and are widely spaced. Shortly after the boundary bank turn right along a track. To the left, through the mature trees, is a large area that has been re-planted with young conifers. Goldcrests may be seen flitting high up in the mature trees.

Shortly reach the junction where you first turned left, and turn left to return to the Forest gate of the car park.

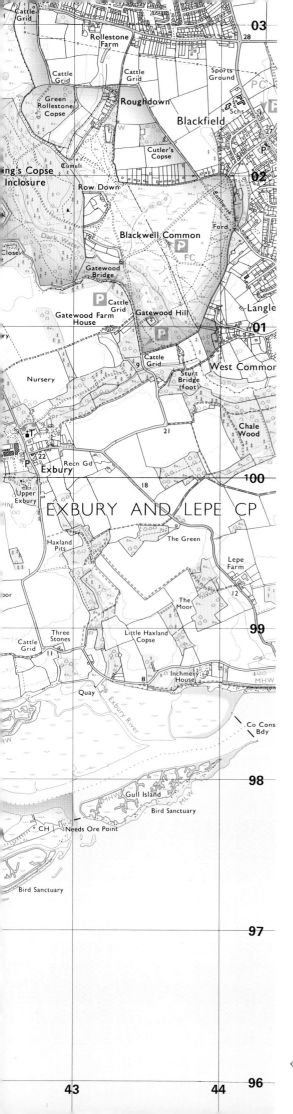

Beaulieu To Bucklers Hard Walk

Allow 90 minutes

This is a way-marked nature trail and leads along paths that are easy to follow. There are no steep gradients.

Leave the car at the car park in Beaulieu village and walk down to the Montagu Arms. Follow the path (sp 'footpath') to the left of the pub. Walk up a metalled road past the fire station. After a short distance reach a stile and begin the walk proper. The path leads through fields and pastures which run down to the Beaulieu River. Among the plants which may be found growing along here in summer are yarrow, ragwort and common centaury. The river is tidal as far as Beaulieu and attracts a variety of waders and waterfowl.

Shortly bear right to follow an inlet of the river and enter a fascinatingly diverse area on the edge of Jarvis's Copse. On the left, by the inlet, there is a miniature marshy area, with rushes, reeds, valerian and willow herbs. Under the lee of the woodland is a drier area rich in meadowland flowers. Among the butterflies that will be seen here are the Peacock and Red Admiral.

Beyond Jarvis's Copse come out into a field and walk beside a hedgerow composed mainly of oak. Follow the trail down to a stile by Bailey's Hard. Follow the nature trail signs beyond Bailey's Hard, and continue the walk along a wide track leading through the mixed woodlands of Keeping Copse. Much of the copse is oakwood, but there is a conifer plantation on the right within which will be seen the distinctive shapes of young cypresses. Nearer to Bucklers Hard the Beaulieu River can be clearly seen through the trees on the left.

Reach a gateway, with the yachts and village of Bucklers Hard ahead. Just past the gateway is an area of mudflats (marked 'dangerous') in which plants such as glasswort and orache may be seen.

Pass Bucklers Hard shipyard and follow the gravel path into the village.

Peacock (top) and Red Admiral butterflies

◁ MAP 14

Index

T

U

Other Ordnance Survey maps of the New Forest.

How to get there with the Routemaster and Tourist Series

Reach the New Forest from London, Birmingham or any other part of South East England with SOUTH EAST ENGLAND, Sheet 9 of the ROUTEMASTER SERIES. Access from Bournemouth, Southampton, Salisbury or Winchester is shown on the NEW FOREST MAP AND GUIDE.

Exploring with the Landranger and Pathfinder Series

Landranger Series
Scale 1:50000 or 1¼ inches to one mile

These maps cover the whole of Britain and are good for local motoring and walking. Each contains tourist information such as parking, picnic places, viewpoints and rights of way. Sheets covering the New Forest are

195 Bournemouth and Purbeck
196 Solent and the Isle of Wight

Pathfinder and Outdoor Leisure Maps
Scale 1:25000 or 2½ inches to one mile

These maps for walkers are the basis of the Outdoor Leisure Map of the New Forest reproduced in this book. Pathfinder maps show the countryside of Britain in great detail, including field boundaries and rights of way in England and Wales. Pathfinders covering parts of the New Forest are
SU 20/30 Lyndhurst
SU 21/31 Totton and part of the New Forest
SU 40/50 Southampton Water and Fareham
SZ 29/39 Lymington